The Crucible of Doubts

*Khomyakov, Dostoevsky, Solov'ev,
In Search of Synthesis,
Four 1929 Works*

by

E. Skobtsova (Mother Maria)

Translated by Fr S. Janos

frsj Publications

The Crucible of Doubts

ISBN: 978-0-9963992-3-4

Library of Congress Control Number: 2016941184

Printed in the United States of America

Printed on acid-free paper.

For information address:

frsj Publications
Fr. Stephen J. Janos
P.O. Box 210
Mohrsville, PA 19541

CONTENTS

IN MEMORY OF MOTHER MARIA

Mother Maria was one of the most remarkable and gifted of Russian women. A representative of her era, she reflected the most characteristic of its currents. She was of a modern sort of soul. She was a poet, a revolutionary and a religious activist.

She belonged to a revolutionary era, she was a social-revolutionary, yet she did not belong to the old type of the revolutionary intelligentsia. Nor was she receptive to the Bol'shevik form of revolution. She had the experience of living through the Russian cultural renaissance at the beginning of the century, and through the Russian poetry of the Symbolist era, she had a close friendship with A. Blok, and shared in the restlessness of that era.

But in the soul of Mother Maria was reflected likewise the religious searchings and trends of the time. She attended lectures at the St. Peterburg Theological Academy. In the emigration she was one of the few with a sympathetic feel for Russian religious philosophy. She actively participated in the Russian Student Christian Movement and departed it, when very rightist tendencies took hold of it.

Mother Maria was by nature very active, always enthusiastic in whatever the matter, but never fully content. Her need for religious activity led her to monasticism. Social motifs always were very strong in her religiosity. She strove towards the creation of a new type of monasticism. The emigrant mentality was rather unreceptive towards this. She aspired in everything towards new forms of activity.

She produced the impression of being an optimist. In her was an exuberance of life. But when a collection of her poetic verse came out, it shew her having moreso a pessimistic and bitter sense of life. Her verses are very remarkable as characteristic of her soul, and

i

likewise also the dramatic poems. Her religiosity was not of the tranquil sort, in it there was something tragic, there was a struggle with God, occasioned by human sufferings, compassion and pity. Resolution of the problems of theodicy did not seem an easy thing for her.

There was moreover a certain feature in Mother Maria, which played an enormous role, and was connected with her tragic end. She had a passionate love for Russia and the Russian people. In the final period of her life, the period of the War, she assumed a tone of passionate patriotism, which took on extreme a form. Her exceptional love for Russia and towards the Russian land and Russian people rendered her often unjust towards the West and Western tendencies. Her world-view could be termed that of a revolutionary Slavophil.

Mother Maria during the time of the Occupation was genuinely a Resistance figure. A source of help to the Jewish. In her was the impression, that she aspired to sacrifice and suffering, she sought to perish on behalf of the Russian people. Her end was heroic. In the German concentration camp she found for herself the religious activity, which actually satisfied her moreso, than in activity in free a world.

N. A. Berdyaev[1]

---

[1] Vide Internet, http://mere-marie.com/life/in-memoriam/, for the Russian version of this article, which does not indicate date nor where originally published.

A. KHOMYAKOV

by E. Skobtsova

I.

Does it make sense in our day to study the philosophic-social schools of the XIX Century? Have not the war and revolution destroyed the old traditions of Russian thought? At present have there not been created totally different experiences? Is not life so very altered, that naught of the old measures is applicable to it?

If this be so, then it would be possible only to approach the study of the Slavophils with purely an historical interest, as towards a memorial of human thought unrelated to contemporary life.

But is such a point of view viable? Is it possible to think that all the events, having taken place in the last decade, are not interwoven by the deepest roots with all the Russian historical past, and the revolution, -- not to remember the relationship? It would seem, that such a view deprives man of the possibility not a little to correctly comprehend all that has occurred.

Events happen in history not by the decree of isolated historical forces, but through the inner laws of the life of a people, and the roots of contemporary processes lie deep within the bulk of its history. Therefore one of the keys for the understanding of them necessitates a search into the study of history and into the study of historical thought of a given people.

In actual fact, -- for our perspectives there has occurred the enormous and completely unique Russian revolution. What explains, that in Russia in particular it has assumed such an unprecedented form? How to comprehend, that approximately one and the same vital circumstances, -- weariness and exhaustion from the war, -- and one and the same social-philosophical doctrine, -- Marxism, -- have produced such strikingly contrary results in Russia and in Germany?

It is certainly completely legitimate to study the common features in the originative processes in these two countries. But it is

3

illegitimate to reject the present at-hand also contrary features, giving an entirely unique hue to these two processes.

Objectivity requires consideration of two kinds of factours in history, -- of those in common for all the simultaneously existing historical process (the war in common, the existence of universally-accepted philosophical positions, common culture, common markets, common economic and labour conditions); -- and of factours, unique however to the separate historical individual: (the influence of the preceding history, national and racial peculiarities, separate particular social attitudes, psychological susceptibility to certain social slogans, historical goals and tasks, geographic conditions, national composition, etc.).

There is an undoubtedly significant role in these and other factours. And objectivity requires an equally attentive attitude towards them, with perhaps one existing reservation: whereas the last decade of Russian social thought has dwelt upon the factours of the former set of conditions, so now particular attention quite inevitably turns round upon factours of the second set, characterising the originality of the historical process in Russia.

It might be expressed thus: the study of this part of the Russian process, which is in common for Russia and for other countries, allowed the Russian Revolution to be predicted with great accuracy. The study however of Russian particularities allows for the comprehension of specific attributes causing events and derives from them the correct conclusion.

By such manner it is possible to affirm, that we stand now in an area of Russian thought fronting an epoch at the edge of historicism, fronting the necessity of a strict and attentive examination of directions, not only of Russian history, but also of the history of Russian social thought.

And on this path there at the first turn rises up before us the school of the Slavophils, imposing such a strong imprint upon the thought of nearly all the XIX Century, and having significant effect on many of the social currents, even those little conscious of this relationship with the Slavophils.

The fundamental significance of the Slavophils consists particularly in this, that they first became interested in the Russian historical process on the side, which makes it unique and dissimilar to the historical processes of other peoples. It is very likely, that in this enthusiasm with Russian peculiarities they went too far, excessively belittling features making Russia kindred with other lands.

But since Slavophil thought was not the only thought in Russia and opposed to them was the school of the Westernisers, sinning at the other extreme, -- a common equilibrium in the understanding of Russian history was maintained. And further on, if it became unbalanced, then in particular it was on the side of the Westernisers, on the side of obliviousness to the way of the Russian people, obliviousness to the way of the Slavophils.

The Slavophils commented on all the fundamental questions contemporary to them in Russia. All the elements having effect upon the psychology of the Russian people were somehow or other studied by them.

At the centre of their understanding stood Orthodoxy, and that prior to them perhaps, the psychological and philosophical aspects had remained entirely undeveloped by Russian thinkers. It might be bold to assert that, prior to Khomyakov, there did not exist in Russia an authentic Orthodox philosophic school, and if Orthodox theologians until then polemicised with Western theologians, then they did this, -- employing in each concrete instance the arguments of Catholicism against Protestantism, or the arguments of Protestantism against Catholicism.

It is even possible to consider, that in the field of theoretical theology the works of Khomyakov played as formative a role for Orthodox consciousness, as the contemporary to him dogma about the infallibility of the pope did for the Catholic consciousness.

The uniqueness of Russian history was thus one of the substantial objectives of the attention of the Slavophils. With particular interest they turned to Muscovite Rus', to the specific peculiarities of its political system and social structure. Alongside the

Westernisers, and after Chaadayev, they for the first time so to speak, "saw into" the authentic Russian history. They were actually the first to turn attention to the significance of community not only for the national economy, but also for the national psyche, -- an issue, which held such decisive significance for all the further advance of Russian social thought.

It is necessary to mention yet one specific peculiarity of the Slavophils: by all their own psychological manner, they themselves as individual people, were representatives of this particular Russian psychological type. For these, -- for each of them in their individuality -- it would be possible to study the Russian national self-consciousness. In this their organic coalescence with the Russian mental temperament, -- secures the genuineness and integrity of their teachings.

According to the Slavophils it is particularly easy to study the unique Russian Christianity. in them we find a peculiar organic democratism, a thirst for sobornost', the predominant unanimity of love over the unity of authority, dislike for the state, for formalism, for external guarantees, the predominance of inner freedom over external legalism, patriarchal nationalism, etc.

It is interesting, that not only would the native Russian Christianity be studied by them, but also the native Russian paganism. They imbued within themselves nearly all of the efficacious strength of the Russian people, and perhaps for the first time gave it a name and verbal embodiment.

In this is their significance and in this is the basic reason for the study of their work.

II.

But before speaking about the teachings and before describing one of the central figures of Slavophilism, -- Alexei Stepanovich Khomyakov, -- it is quite necessary to sketch out the appearance of the epoch that was contemporaneous to him.

The epoch of Chaadayev, Granovsky, Hertsen, Bakunin, Khomyakov, the Kireevskys, the Aksakovs: this was an until then unprecedented period in the history of Russian thought.

In actual fact, -- the traditions of Muscovite Rus' had dissipated behind them, changed and altered so far as to be unrecognisable by the time of the reform of Peter. The way path back to it forbidden, its culture almost forgotten, it was screened off, obliterated. Immediately atop its shoulders there stood the XVIII Century, -- a very strange and unexpected period of Russian history, the period of a great schism in Russian culture, the blossoming of Western ideas, customs, fashions, the splendid century of Catherine, having nearly colonised the savage Russian plains, engrafting onto it the laws of Montesquieu and the Western free-thinking of Diderot.

It seems, -- possibly bold to assert, -- if the Russian Revolution, in the sense of change of existing economic and legal attitudes, resulted in the year 1917, -- then there had preceded it in the field of cultural experiences and spiritual tendencies some revolution, -- the revolution of the first half of the XIX Century, -- altering thus the rough grafting of the Petrine tradition, weaning Russian thinkers off from the eternal awareness of Western life shewn them by the exertions of Peter, turning round their "face towards Russia". This epoch is one of the more interesting and indicative in Russian history, -- if we do not enter into how it developes, then we do not enter into the modern time, -- since the primary roots of the majority of teachings contemporaneous to us are actually located within it.

On its external side this epoch is characterised by the reign of Nicholas I. The creative exertions of Peter were long since disintegrated. Pompously luxuriant, but in essence foreign to the Russian people, the monarchy of Catherine was already of dim visage. Alexander's troops had made the rounds of Europe and returned home, bringing about simultaneously the radical ideas of the Decembrists, a nurturing of the philosophies of revolutionary France, but also the mysticism of a Bible society, of the Quakers, and of

French-masonry, and Baroness Krudener, -- all the vivid colour of German romanticism, arisen upon Protestant fermentations.

Russian thought was not only imbued with Western ideas, -- it was drenched in them.

And perhaps the fundamental meaning of the reign of Nicholas consists particularly in this, that it was impossible to go farther upon this path, it was impossible to live because of the foreign ideas and the foreign culture. Therefore the official Russian culture became ossified, gelled in its own cold lustre, contorted in an uniform, gasping in splendid parades.

And organically in turn there began to grow another culture, striving to perceive its own connection not with the West, but with its own particular people.

No one perhaps better than Hertsen expressed the torments of the developing process. And no one better than he defined the appearing of new forces on the scene and their correlation.

At that time "the Russia of the future -- says he, -- existed exclusively amidst several young boys, of such extent insignificant and unremarkable, allowed sufficiently a space for them between the soles of aristocratic jack-boots and the earth, -- and in them was the legacy of 14 December, the legacy of the social-human sciences and of the purely national Rus'."

It is necessary to say that Hertsen was quite accurate in his formulation of the three legacies, -- these insignificant boys, having later on become representatives of Russian culture, further having splintered according to the aspect perceived by them endowing the legacy, -- they themselves defined the further course of Russian thought, and in contrast to the XVIII Century, they imparted to all the coming epoch of Russian thought its tensioned and at the same time organic character.

At present it is difficult to account for and comprehend the burden which they took upon themselves, -- an explosive burden with strange traditions, created on the vacant spot of Russian national self-consciousness, laying the foundation for the history of the Russian intelligentsia.

Hertsen has passages, referring to him personally and to his ideological opponents, characterising this burden with precise clarity.

Here they are:

"For what are we waken up early? To go to sleep, like everything around."

"Our condition is hopeless and our deed desperate suffering."

"My shoulders ache, but still they carry. Do a future people catch hold of, do they appreciate all the terror, all the tragic side of our existence? And amidst that in our sufferings, -- nigh from which is bred their happiness. Do they catch hold of why we laggards have all the pleasures, drink wine and suchlike? Why the hands are not put to great work, why during moments of pleasure melancholia is not forgotten? Let them dwell with thought and with grief before the stone, under which we are fallen asleep: we have deserved their grief."

And he says this not only about his like-minded associates, but about all his generation.

Here is how he characterises the Slavophil Kireevsky, his ideological opponent: "He suffers, and knows, that he suffers, and he wants to suffer, not reckoning in truth to put down the burdensome and dark cross, imposed by fate upon him."

This cross, burdensome and dark, weighs down upon the entire generation: new forces awaken, Russian thought struggles forth onto new paths, -- and those, who began the new way, -- were certainly the doomed.

And it may be that variously they sensed this doom. Here then Hertsen characterises the approaches to the future by Chaadayev and by the Slavophils.

"From Chaadayev there glimmers weakly the possibility of salvation of the person, but not the nation. From the Slavophils the thought about the destruction of persons in the grips of the contemporary era is clearly overlooked, but there is faith in the salvation of the people."

The selected passage but suffices to acutely feel the tension of the era and the difficulty, before which stood the young independent Russian thought.

Chaadayev was the instigator. He first set forth the question about this difficulty.

"The letter of Chaadayev, -- says Hertsen, -- was for his generation the final word, the border-line. Here was a shot, heard in the dark night. Whether it foundered and announced destruction, whether it was a signal, a cry for help, an announcement about the morning or that a morning would not be, -- all variously, -- was of necessity awakened."

What was this final word he announced? What was necessary to start from that border-line? And finally, -- did Chaadayev announce a morning or that there would not be a morning.

We turn to him because he, -- at the beginning of the era, -- asked as it were the question, upon which then was given answer variously from the lips of all the representative sides.

"In Moscow they guide every foreigner to see a large cannon and a large bell, -- a cannon, from which it is impossible to shoot, and the bell, which fell down before it rang. A wondrous city, in which the remarkable is distinguished by absurdity. Or might it be this great bell without a tongue, -- is an hieroglyph, expressing for this huge dumb land, peopled by a tribe calling itself Slavic, as though surprised that it possesses the word human."

In these words, -- there is irony and more.

Suchlike irony permeates the dialogue of Hertsen with the Slavophils:

They affirm: "Moscow, -- is the capital of the Russian people, and Peterburg -- is only the residence of the Russian emperor."

But Hertsen, agreeing with them, says: "And observe, how far this distinction goes: in Moscow they lock you up in the round-house, and in Peterburg they inform on at the guard-house."

But all these quotes concern mainly characteristics of the state of things contemporary to them.

Amidst them perhaps it is not the contemporary, but the past, that manifests in the given instance the cause of all the bewilderment and suffering of Chaadayev. He as it were did discover Russian history, it was for him still sealed up, it was all absorbed and dissolved in the non-Russian XVIII Century.

The characteristics ascribed by him to the Russian past are certainly now for us strange and odd. But if now we see that in these characteristics he was mistaken, then from the other side they show for us with incontestable testimony, what a deep split the XVIII Century inflicted upon the body of the Russian people, how all the old sources were forgotten, how they came to build literally upon a bare place.

It is necessary to quote his words about the Russian past in entirety, since they indicate for us very accurately all the difficulty standing in the way of the Slavophils, when they sought out the roots of Russian organic life. Chaadayev is indeed somewhat older than the primary Slavophil generation, but meanwhile except for a wasteland he cannot be separated from their ranks.

"At first we have wild barbarism, then crude ignorance, then grim and humiliating foreign rule, the spirit of which our national authority inherited, -- such was the sad history of our youth. The epoch of our social life was filled with a dim and obscure existence, personal initiative and energy animated none save evil-doers, nothing was mitigated save slavery. Take a look at all our living through the centuries, all our occupying of space, -- you will find no single pleasant recollection, nor graceful images in the memory of the people, nor any respectable memorial, which would speak to us powerfully about the past".

"What did we do about that time, when in the conflict between the energetic barbarism of the northern nations with the profound thought of Christianity there was formed the house of contemporary civilisation? Urged on by our bad judgment, we turned for our moral regulation towards the wretched Byzantium, deeply scorned by these nations, which should have to lay at the foundation of our upbringing. By the will of a certain honour-loving Photios there was rejected the universal brotherhood of this family of nations that just barely was. In Europe a vivifying principle of unity animated everything. Not having partaken of this wonder-working source, we fell victim to conquest. And furthermore the new destiny of the human race is accomplished in spite of us".

And therefore the effort of Peter -- is the greatest blessing. "He perceived, that standing face to face with the old European civilisation, which is the final expression of all the previous civilisations, that not for it are we choked in history and not for it are we dragged through the chaos of national prejudices through the dug-down ruts of native traditions, but that we ought by the free impulse of our inner strength to seize hold of our destiny. He transferred to us the West complete, what the centuries had made it, and gave us its history for history, all its future for the future".

And finally: "We belong to the list of those nations, which as it were do not enter into the constituting of mankind, and they exist only so as to give the world some important lesson".

True, side by side with this Chaadayev says: "You know, I have this view, that Russia is summoned to a not for certain intellectual deed. Its task is to give at its own time a resolution to all the questions arousing controversy in Europe. Positioned outside that impulsive movement which minds bring there, it received for its lot to give in its own time the resolution of the human enigma".

"Everything great proceeds from the wilderness".

Certainly we might now very precisely analyse all the elements contained in these words.

And Hertsen is correct, characterising these frames of mind thus: "And if when at the moment of endless pain, they cursed the ungrateful, harsh parental home, then indeed this one strengthening upon the mind they did not hear in their cursings of the blessing".

But it is not this, it is not the endless pain even, that ought to make us interested in the words of Chaadayev.

The very basis, that is heard in them -- this is a summoning. They are by no means an answer. They are only the boundlessly sharpened question, -- the question about the Russian destiny.

And upon this question, in essence set forth not by Chaadayev alone, but by all the aggregate of Russian historical conditions, by the tense and congealed greatness to which the Russia of his time had arrived at, -- it was impossible to be silent.

Chaadayev's shot was heard, -- actually all the Russia of his time was abroad the frontier, -- "the announcement about morning or about, that morning would not be". "It was necessary to be asleep", -- to be asleep and to answer.

And we know the endless answers, with which the XIX Century was filled. Particularly its basic content, -- this torment of Russian thought about its own Russian destiny, a thirst to guess at its mysterious signs, to discern the pointing out of its way, to comprehend itself. And perhaps it would be simple to make an endless register of such answers, attempts to make self-definition. The final attempts reach the present day.

But howsoever they might be varied, it is possible in them to derive according to precise features the acknowledged classification.

Slavophilism and Westernism, the dynamic and the static, historicism and economism, populism and marxism, the neo-Slavophilism and the neo-Westernism, -- these are all famous contrary positions, characterising Russian thought upon the pathways of its self-definition.

And before proceeding to the first attempt of an wholistic positional answer to Chaadayev's question, -- to the attempt of the Slavophils and Khomyakov in particular, -- it is necessary to characterise the correlation with the other current, -- in particular with Hertsen, who was on the one hand undoubtedly much keener than the Slavophils, but on the other, -- he did not have their pathos of construct and creativity. His was a pathos of repulsion, criticism, and destruction.

Often his view on Russian history coincides with Chaadayev:

"The bell of Novgorod the Eternal was merely transformed into a cannon by Peter, and examined alongside with the bell-tower of Ivan Vasilevich. A strong state was only consolidated by the revision under Peter, but it was introduced by Godunov. The knout, rods, whips appear far earlier than gauntlets and saber-blows".

"Askold and Dir were the only decent people from all those issuing from Rurik. They took their boats indeed and went from them on foot into Kiev. The single period in Russian history, which does not read terribly nor sadly, -- this is the Kievan period".

Hertsen himself also provides extensive material for the characteristics of Slavophilism and of his attitude towards it:

On the first volley he very originally ascertains its ancestry:

"The executed, the quartered, those hung upon the jagged-teeth of the Kremlin and there shot by Menshikov and other tsarist boy-soldiers in the guise of the raging streltsi, the poisoning within the raveling twist of the Peterburg fortress in the guise of the tsarevich Aleksei, it appears, like a detachment of Dolgoruki under Peter II, like the enmity toward the Germans under Byron, like Pugachev under Catherine II, like Catherine herself, -- the Orthodox Germaness under the Prussian Holstein Peter III, -- like Elizabeth, relying on the Slavophils of that time in order to sit upon the throne. All the schismatics, -- were Slavophils. All the white and the black of the clergy, -- were Slavophils. Soldiers, Barclay de Tolle needing a change for his German family, were predecessors of Khomyakov and his companions".

But with them Hertsen cultivates a strange attitude: they became friend-enemies.

"Yes, we were antagonists, but very strangely so. We had a certain love, but not identical. In the early years they were and we were empassioned of a certain strong, unaccountable, philosophical dread feeling, -- a feeling of boundless, all-embracing love for the Russian people. And we, like Janus or like the double-headed eagle, considered the various sides, at that time, like a single heart beat. They bore all love, all tenderness towards the oppressed mother. In their room it was stuffy for us. All the dark faces from behind silver beards ... we knew, that theirs were not bright recollections, -- we both knew, that their happiness ahead, that beneathe it an embryo beats its heart, -- this is our young brother, to whom we cede precedence without a lentil".

"For them a tradition was necessary, a past, -- for us it was to desire to separate Russia from it".

"They set out to seek the living Rus' in the chronicles, just as Mary Magdalene sought Jesus in the tomb".

"For them the Russian people is pre-eminently Orthodox, ie. closest to everything heavenly; for us it is pre-eminently social, ie. much closer to everything earthly".

"Translating from an apocalyptic language for us and illumining by light of day, that what at Khomyakov's was illuminated by a chandelier, I saw clearly, how in many similar ways we perceived the western question".

But alongside with this:

"We saw in their teaching a new oil anointing the tsar, a new flail lain upon thought, a new subjugation of conscience by the servile Byzantine church. Their iconographic ideals and the smoke of the incense hindered us in examining the national way of life, and the principles of village life. Their treasure perhaps is concealed in church utensils of ancient work, but the value of it then was not in the vessel nor in the form. Slavyanism existed from the time of the shaving of the first beard by Peter I."

A finally a last quotation:

"History, as a movement of mankind towards liberation and self-awareness, does not exist for the Slavophils. They say that the fruit of European life ripened in the Slavic world, that Europe, having attained to science, is the negation of the existing, the finally providential future in questions of socialism and communism, -- is itself finished, and that the Slavic world, -- is the soil of a sympathetic, organic development for the future. The Slavophils, believing in a dream-like future, though they understand the present, but rejoicing in the future they are at peace with it, -- their happiness".

I think, that the included quotations, -- the testimony of so outstanding a contemporary, the friend-enemy Hertsen, is sufficient in order to feel the tense atmosphere of the controversies in the first half of the XIX Century.

After a long hibernation, after a strange period of history, Russian thought awoke and at first it was frightened of the surroundings. In actual fact, -- at its base, was the traditional past, of which a great century closes. In reality there were no reminiscences. Every substantive idea was rooted in Western ideas. The unique face of Russian culture was split and shredded. Life coursed along several channels. The capital, the court and the nobility maintained Prusso-Holstein mannerisms, attired in their pre-revolutionary Versailles pompousness, and otherwise the provincial regions, the countryside, all the Russian expanse was maintained somehow escaping the roots of the Moscow tsardom.

What to comprehend, as proper? What to perceive as uniquely genuine, not only by chance what we have preserved, but the way of life, the organic connections of all sides of Russian culture?

And indeed is there such a genuine Russian principle, capable to give life a further history?

Chaadayev called this into question. And if sometimes he arrived at the conclusion that afront Russia lay a great pathway, then it is only on the basis that everything great proceeds from the wilderness.

Hertsen at first indeed called into question the Russian destiny and he was inclined to look to the West. But finding himself there, stifled by European phillistinism, he came nigh to the view of the Slavophils on Russian originality.

But repelled by the existing order of things, he was by inclination a revolutionary, so as to construct an organic system of the correlations of Russian life.

The first attempt at such a construct belonged to the Slavophils. It seems that here Hertsen was not correct in his characteristics: in particular the aspiration to find living Rus' in the chronicles created what in many respects of their teachings now at present bears in itself the seal of contemporaneity.

But their chief and indisputable service is in this, that they concentrated the basic attention of their investigation at the centre of Russian spiritual life, -- on Orthodoxy.

III.

One of the central figures of Slavophilism was Aleksei Stepanovich Khomyakov.

Not only in what he wrote, but also in all his spiritual aspect, is bespoken those traits characteristic of the Slavophils: an organic unity with the Russian national psychology and an extraordinary integrity of world-concept.

Khomyakov wrote much and on very diverse questions. But on all his works lies the seal of a single purpose, they are all marked by an original and organic wholeness. Neither the time of inscription, nor the theme, breaks the connections with a certain spiritual core of all his existence.

A numerical majority of his works are devoted to historical questions, but very interesting and very significant there needs to be considered his purely theological works, devoted to the question about the Orthodox concept of the nature of the Church.

For this, the more vividly demonstrate the integrity of Khomyakov's world-concept, it is necessary first of all to dwell upon his philosophy of history, from which inevitably flow all his other positions. --

For Khomyakov, the historical process is the development of a living, concrete national organism. This national organism, like every other, has its own individual peculiarity and does not become fused together in an admixture with other organisms.

An impelling factour in the history of a people appears to be its faith. He defines it like a psychological individuality, it establishes the goal of its historical process, and it chooses the form of realisation of this goal. To comprehend the particularity of faith of a given people, -- this is to comprehend all its inner essence.

From another side the historical process appears always as the conflict of two principles, -- freedom and necessity, -- in other words, -- spirit and matter. Free spirit is a creative principle in history, for which it is appropriate to overcome the stagnation of matter and the law of necessity in which matter sojourns.

And the type of faith, the peculiarity of religious attitude towards the world mainly defines how a nation perceives these two principles in the historical process.

In accord with this Khomyakov divides all religions into Kushite or Iranian.

Kushitism, -- this is the religion of necessity. It determines by itself the power and force of matter over the free creative spirit. Magicism appears its characteristic manifestation.

Iranism, -- is a religion of freedom, a religion of the creative spirit, of a conquering the stagnation of matter, of overcoming necessity.

All pagan religions appear mainly as the manifestation of Kushitism. Judaism needs be considered the first historical example of Iranism.

Kushitism in turn branches into one of its parts, -- in Shivaism, -- it worships the sovereignty of matter, it definitively departs from the awareness and benevolence of spirit. Another current of Kushitism, -- is Buddhism, -- this is the worship of enslaved spirit, a spirit which inevitably is subservient to materiality and does not possess freedom.

The Kushite principle defines not only religions, but also very diverse philosophic systems. Khomyakov discerns it in the Phoenician religion, in Buddhism, in Ophite snake-worshippers, in materialism, in his contemporary day, in Hegel.

Moreover, -- Khomyakov considers that Kushitism has triumphed in Catholicism, and this distorted its Christian principle, which appears utmost an Iranian principle.

From the perspective of this criteria and another force, having decisive significance in the historical destinies of Europe, -- Germanism, -- is thus situated wholly in the power of the Kushite principle. The Germanic spirit, -- this is a spirit of conquest. It split the European community into conquerors and conquered.

And perhaps nowhere in the world is there expressed so powerfully the genuine Iranian principle, as in the fundamental qualities of the Russian people. From here emanates the stateless character of all the Slavs in general, -- bearers of the Iranian spirit, -- from here also is an organic Russian democratism, from here is the power of the communal principle, the principle of Sobornost', grounded on freedom. The Russian church is foreign to Roman imperialism, the Russian man is not a conqueror, but rather a peaceful agriculturalist.

In brief, if in the world there exists a most complete embodiment of the Iranian spirit, then this particularly is in the Russian people. The natural Christian qualities of the Russian soul unite harmoniously with the teachings of the Orthodox Church.

III.

From the perspective of the Iranian principle, -- of the creativity of free spirit over the stagnation of matter and over the laws of necessity, -- Khomyakov also arrives at his teaching about society and the state. And in the relationship of the Russian people to the state, he again likewise examines its relation to Iranism.

Khomyakov was not only himself an anti-statist, -- he attributes anti-statism to the psychology of all the Russian people.

The state for him, -- is a dead mechanism, covering the living social organism of the people. And where there is the mechanism, there is always necessity. Only for an organism is there an attributive freedom.

Therefore the hero and chief actualising personage of the historical process is not the state, but rather the people. The state is a dead mechanical shell, -- an encasing, -- of the living manifestation of the national spirit. The state is only an object of national creativity, -- its subject and creator, is manifest as the people. Every exaggeration of the significance of the state is an exaggeration of necessity and a diminuation of the significance of the free creative spirit.

Power primordially appertains to the people and it is free to direct it according to its discretion, since it is an authentic and unique subject of the historical process.

Thus, -- in the opinion of Khomyakov, -- is the perception of state and Russian people. On this basis he therefore is very little a statist, -- he is even simply an anarchist.

What for the Russian people was the creation of autocracy by it, as distinct from Western absolutism? It was for it a genuine spiritual liberation from politics, -- that sphere of life, to which it attributed such little significance.

In autocracy is expressed the political asceticism of the people. Psychologically it is bound up with the stateless anarchist spirit of the people. In it, it sets itself free from the necessary, but emburdening it, of state duties.

The fundamental formula of Russian autocratic monarchy is thus: "Russian autocratic monarchy is the statism of a stateless people".

But if the Russian people is not a state in the genuine sense of the word, of its vocation, then the vocation of the social in it is very strong. The absence of the one absolutely does not predicate the absence of the other.

For the self-arrangement, for the inner democratic resolution of social questions the Russian people has a very great proclivity.

It would be correct to say, that the vocation of the Russian people is not state-political, but familial-existential. And then the fundamental social unit of the Russian people mustneeds be accounted the family. And indeed the family in essence ought to be the cell of organic society.

Further, by way of realisation of its own social-economic interests, families are associated within patriarchal rural communities, actualised on democratic principles, -- on principles of self-management, -- its own right to the land, to work, bearing in itself all social rights and duties.

It is necessary to note, that for Khomyakov the voice of such social sobornost'/collectivity offered a more valuable and notable seal of specific soborno-collective wisdom, compared with the voices and opinions of individual people... The "mir/village-commune" and the resolution of the "mir/village-commune" for him is not only a resolution of the individuals comprising its visage, but also the resolution of a certain soborno-collective body, manifest as a living organism and actualised by particular psychological laws.

Such is the second social cell bestowing an unique character to Russian history.

Finally, the completive social organism appears to be the zemschina/land-commune, coalescing within itself all the obschina/community. To it appertains the voice of the land, the voice of all the people. It ought to determine the national pathway, and to a remarkable degree it is unerring in the area of resolution of social questions. And in any event indeed it is not able to betray the fundamental psychological lifestyle of the Russian people, since it is organically conjoined with it.

The zemschina/land-commune is not divided into classes, -- the zemschina is a sobornost'/collectivity of all the people.

From this there issues forth the idea of the zemsky Duma / land Council, of the Zemsky Sobor.

It is necessary not to presume, that in this concept Khomyakov has incorporated the principle of West-European parliamentarism. No, in European parliamentarism there exists the yearning of the nation for a sharing in power. Parliament defines itself as the national right to power.

Khomyakov's Duma or Sobor/Assemblage is based first off on a national aversion to power, on national anarchism. In essence it is the zemschina, speaking within the Duma, that is the bearer of power. But, since the nation does not possess any of the pathos of power, it then cedes it to the autocratic tsar, whose obligation, -- is not formal, but in virtue of the quite moral nature of his service, -- in regard with the zemschina, -- with the unerringly precise voice of all the nation.

In such manner the ideal social structure of the Russian state is presented by Khomyakov thus: a national patriarchal monarchy, it rests in the broadly developed village obschina, which expresses itself and its will in the Zemsky/Land Duma.

Actually it is not only the Sovereign power of the Russian people that was delegated to the tsar. It even gave to the tsar its power in churchly matters. And the tsar is the representative of the nation to the church. (But certainly by no means is he the secular head of the Church).

The Church and the state are bound together in Russian history not by caesaro-papism, as many mistakenly presuppose, thereby not accounting it a genuine matter of consequence, -- but by the people, which delegated to the tsar his two functions, -- wielding of power and representation to the Church.

"The Sovereign is head of the nation in church matters, but in no instance is he head of the Church"...

IV.

Here is this very hero of the historical process, the acting fashioner of its own history, -- the Russian people, -- in all its experiences and forms, that primarily occupies the thought of Khomyakov.

And in his understanding of the Russian people there intersect two interesting and original concepts, later on playing an exceptional role in the two contrary wings of Russian social-thought: populism and nationalism.

The usual classical examples of Russian nationalism occur always as right-wing social thought and it relies upon chauvinism in the border-lands. Nationalism in Russia cloaked itself mostly in the aggressive sovereignty-rights and territorial pretensions of the Russian empire.

Populism, -- the fruition of the thought of the left, the revolutionary circles of Russian society, -- was little interested in state pretensions to empire and it deciphered itself not in governmental, but rather in social maximalism. It sought after the national labour truth in that obschina/community, in those unique social peculiarities of Russian existence, wherein Khomyakov sought after his truth.

In no other language is there such a delineation between the inner nuances of the words: natsia (nation) and narod (nation/native-populace) [Translator note: the word "na-rod" linguistically signifies "born-within hence native-to family/kin/tribe/country"]. In no other language do these concepts lead to the antagonistic word-images: natsionalizm/nationalism and narodnichestvo/populism.

In Russia not only these concepts, but also the truth, contained in each of them, -- was harshly antagonistic to each other.

Which was Khomyakov, a narodnik/populist or a nationalist? In the precise meaning which these words later formed, he was neither the one nor the other. For the nationalist he did not support sovereignty, for the populist, -- he was deficient of social radicalism.

But undoubtedly to a remarkable degree these two concepts intersected and conjoined within him.

And the people, as such, was for him the bearer of a certain genuine truth of its own, variously reflected in the separate planes of national life.

In the area of religion the people confessed not an obscured but rather the true Christianity, -- the Orthodox faith.

In the area of the social it erected its own manner of life upon the genuine "secular" sobornost'/collectivity, in the principle of "obschina/communality".

In the area of the state-political he prudently refrained from unbearable political ties and he posited the autocracy, -- that this is the statism of a stateless people.

Searching through all the distinct peculiarities of the Russian people, Khomyakov proceeds to the conclusion of what the people is, -- it is a messianic people, having a religious and universal vocation. And the purpose of this calling cannot in any way be to revere the ideal of the might of empire. The purpose of this calling, -- is rather the ideal of Holy Rus'.

The Russian people is conscious of this its vocation and in such purport senses itself the foremost people in the world. And in line with this, it perceives that this primacy obligates it to a primacy in humility. In order to realise its own national religious calling, the Russian people ought simultaneously to be filled with audacity and penitence. It ought to scourge its sins, which primarily are situated in the political.

The task of the Russian people, its universal and religious mission, the meaning of its vocation, -- is contained within the creative integrity of life, in realised community, in the imbuing with the religious principle, in the annulling of that secular world-concept, which corrupts the contemporary culture of Europe.

V.

And here we come to the purely philosophical and metaphysical constructs of the Slavophils. In this area thus again the works of Khomyakov are the most interesting. He conceived of his own philosophy, as the beginning of a new era in world-conceptualisation. The time was come to put an end to the abstract philosophy of the West, the time was come to surmount the cult of intellect, the cult of abstract rationality.

In particular it is necessary to overcome the abstract idealism of Hegel by an idealism of the concrete, it is necessary to lay bare its fundamental fault consisting in this, that it adopts rationality in place of integrality of spirit and it replaces the concept of integral spirit with the concept of rationality. This bespeaks its Kushitism, the impossibility of an Iranian, genuine assimilation of the biddings of the free spirit.

Slavophil philosophy desires to be philosophy of the integral life of the spirit.

Khomyakov takes into account that the comprehension of the existing is given only within the multi-imaged fulness of life. And for him the defect of German idealist philosophy became by its nature pre-determined, by that it religiously shews itself the product of

Protestantism, -- of creed-confession, of a personal basis and impossible wholeness.

Authentic spiritual wholeness, the understanding of reason, as of a creative and willing Logos, -- this only have the Orthodox preserved. And on this basis however, upon the soil of Orthodoxy might be fashioned the present philosophy of the spirit.

And Slavophil philosophy consciously did turn towards religious nourishment.

Slavophil philosophy thought of itself as Orthodox philosophy. Slavophil gnosseology is Church gnosseology.

The quite characteristic features of the philosophical speculations of Khomyakov shew first-off an affirmation of the unity of subject and object, and a denial of their dissection, a splitting so characteristic to Western thought.

Furthermore, authentic philosophy ought to be a philosophy of action, -- for it there ought not to be the accepted intellectualism of the West.

It ought to disclose the sameness of knowledge and faith, -- two forms of world-comprehension, rooted in equal extent within the verymost integral spirit.

The centre of Khomyakov's gnosseology, -- is the teaching about volitional reason and reasonal will.

Finally, there is in his philosophy a certain position, showing the link between the expressions of his historico-social character and the purely theological theoretics about the nature of the Church.

For him the organic individual consciousness is powerless to apprehend the existing. Isolated within its own organicity and its own environs, it is not able to apprehend this organicity. There is accessible for it however a partial perception of the existing. Therefore every philosophy, based upon individual consciousness, inevitably is doomed to result in the dead-end of intellectualism, of subjective idealism, etc.

Authentic apprehension of the existing is accessible only to the soborno-collective consciousness of people. Collective consciousness is however not the summa of the constituative assemblage of individual consciousnesses. It is more than this summa and it organically surmounts its exclusiveness and isolation in its own perceived organicity.

Soborno-collective consciousness manifests itself as Church consciousness. By such manner only of the Church is there an attributive true philosophy, only the Church in all its various manifestations can presume to the comprehending of the existing.

In this position we recognise to a certain degree his former assertion of the authenticity and truth of the voice "of the world", of "obschina/community", of a circular process. Just as the obschina/community, intertwining the worldly and legal needs of its members, possesses a greater inner signification in its correct-perceptions than an isolated man, -- so then on an higher plane, -- in the area of perception, -- the soborno-collective voice possesses greater precedence than by comparison with a voice of separative individualism.

All the world in its own ideal, on all its levels in which it is manifest, originating from the simple and straight-forward plane of the everyday and labouring life of people, and ending with the pinnacles of the religious life of the spirit, -- ought to be established upon the soborno-collective principle, destroying at the roots intellectualism and rationalism and revealing the possibility to manifest itself with all the qualities and particularities of the integral spirit.

From here results also a quite fundamental teaching of Khomyakov, -- the Teaching about the Church. But before moving on to it, it is necessary to digress upon his opinions about other Christian confessions of belief, and impairments and distortions impeding the idea of integral spirit.

6.

What was the history of the Schism? What occurred between Patriarch Photios and Pope Nicholas? What sundered the before-then unique unity of love of the Church?

Khomyakov thought that it was not dogmatic divergences that were the central event defining the falling-away of the West from the unity of the OEcumenical Church, and that it was not some historical facts, making impossible further communality of West and East.

The defining cause and center of everything was a betrayal of the love of Christ, happening in the West. The unity of the love was transgressed, -- and this defined everything.

Even long before the Schism, the local Spanish Church had introduced into the teaching of the Symbol of Faith the word "filioque/and-of-the-son". (It asserted the procession of the Holy Spirit not only from the Father, but also from the Son, -- "Who from the Father and the Son -- filioque -- proceedeth"). The local Spanish tradition accepted, as obligatory, this altered reading, and it gradually spread beyond the region of Spain.

In this there was, certainly, already a guarantee of great and substantial divergences further on. But in essence the Church possessed the true and tested means not to admit any of the fatal consequences from this chance deviation of one of the provinces of the Church.

It would have sufficed to lay forth the question about the filioque for examination by an OEcumenical Council, and it would be able to quite authoritatively and fully to resolve it, referring to the text of Holy Scripture and corroborating by the very positions of Holy Tradition. Such a resolution of the question is required by this unity of love, which shews itself central to the living organism of the Church.

In place of this, Pope Nicholas misappropriated the partial Western opinion as correct in his independent decision of a dogmatic question, not having reckoned with the opinion of all the OEcumenical Church, -- of all the Body of Christ.

"By his action, ie. by the arbitrary changing of the Symbol/Creed, the Roman world declared that in its eyes all the East, -- is an helot-slave in matters of faith. The right of deciding dogmatic questions was misappropriated by a regional church".

Outside of love, the universal Church does not have communality with the local churches, -- it does not know some different quality of obschenie/communality.

And this act of the West, transgressing the oneness of love, tears it asunder from the OEcumenical Church and predetermines the inevitability of further deepening of schism. Everything subsequent logically issues forth from this act.

"Genuine love is not able to be preserved, where love is grown scarce".

The law of love was replaced by utilitarianism and rationalism.

And in essence this act of the Western Church contained within itself the full legitimising of Protestantism. "In Catholicism ripened the seed of the Reformation. The Western Church turned man himself into a slave and the consequence of this was to make in him himself the arbitrator".

In actual fact: once it withdrew from unified soborno-collective life with all the OEcumenical Church, Catholicism withdrew from the correct understanding of the mystical existence of the ecclesiastic body. In principle it accepted the fortuitous criterion of human reason in matters of faith, and this very thing determined the relativeness of this criterion.

For Catholicism in the final reckoning the dogma became necessary about the infallibility of the pope, so as somehow to fill in the spot, occupied formerly by the concept of the infallibility of the Church in its integral-incorporativeness. This dogma is no less rationalised, than the affirmation of Protestantism, negating the Church. The difference here is one only of degrees and tendencies.

With equal intensity both in Catholicism and in Protestantism there is actualised a principle of utmost rationalism, bereft of the wholeness of spirit. And if in Protestantism rationalism is idealicised, then in Catholicism this rationalism is materialicised. In this only is the difference between them.

Catholicism started to reject dogma, as a living tradition of all the universal Church, and replaced it with the tradition of the local church. Protestantism went further, and in its rejection of dogma as living tradition, it affirmed tradition as already altogether outside-the-church and fortuitous.

By such means the first step, leading to the schism, predetermined further on the external-church solitude of Western man, and it made even his prayer juridical-rationalist.

Having withdrawn from the one genuine basis of religious Christian life, -- from the basis of unity in love, -- and having split into two hostile camps within itself, -- Protestantism and Catholicism, -- the West in all its own internecine polemics moreso does not concern itself with the genuine roots of religious life but all the time wanders about upon superficialities.

All the disputes about the significance of supra-necessary merits, about the strength and meaning of prayer, about the correlation of faith and good deeds, -- always they are explained by a rooted-in incorrectness in the proposing of questions, and these very contrary affirmations in this area are equally far from the true positions of the Church, such that they are imbued thoroughly with rationalism and legalism.

The majority of these questions simply do not exist, and even if it exists, then it is easily resolved on the basis of the central command of love, permeating the Church.

From the indissoluble inner bonds of Protestantism and Catholicism it inevitably appears, that Protestantism is not able to spread beyond its boundary with the Catholic world. The sin of Protestantism manifests itself wholly as the sin of Catholicism. In it was expressed the fundamental impairment of Catholic love and Catholic unity.

They are simultaneously interwoven and simultaneously inevitable.

And at present it is clear that Orthodoxy, not suffering the sickness of rationalism and juridicism, -- does not permit of a Protestant incursion.

Before which, in passing over to the definition of the genuine universal meaning of the Church given by Orthodoxy, it is interesting to note, how Khomyakov characterises the contrary views of East and West on certain questions.

"The wisdom of the East teaches about the command of love; the folly of the West, -- teaches about the power and the gift of love."

"We know, that the Church does not seek after Christ, as the Protestants seek after Him, but rather it is commanded by Him, and possesses and accepts Him constantly, not putting itself forth as the external symbol of Christ, as produced by the belief of the Romans."

"The grit does not receive new being from the heap, on which it is flung by chance. Such is man in Protestantism.

The brick situated in a wall, by no means changes itself nor improves itself from the place, assigned it by the bevel of the stone-mason. Such is man in Romanism.

But all the parts of the corpus, by comprising the body, makes it an integral part of its organism, and itself receives from it new meaning and new life. Such is man in Orthodoxy".

"Three voices louder than others are heard in Europe: "Obey and believe in my decrees" -- says Rome. "Be free and strive to fashion yourself some sort of faith" -- this say Protestants. But the Church invokes to its own: "Let us love one another so that with oneness of mind we may confess, -- Father and Son and Holy Spirit".

From these examples we see how Khomyakov defines the essential difference of Orthodoxy and the Western confessions.

The difference here is in the very understanding of spiritual life, in the quite mystical attitude towards the Church and towards being present within it.

And in this, in how he deepens the very setting of the question, and in that answer which he gives to it, is reflected a fundamental feature of the religiosity of Khomyakov, venturing Samarin to call him the first Russian Orthodox theologian.

7.

Having turned away from the West and having polemicised with it, Khomyakov sets forth the fundamental teaching about true sobornost'/collectivity, confessed by the Orthodox Church.

The original starting point availing him was the circulative epistle of the Eastern Patriarchs in the year 1848, written in the form of an answer to Pope Pius IX upon the first attempts by Rome to promulgate the dogma about the infallibility of the pope.

This epistle includes within it the following definition of the organ of Church infallibility:

"Infallibility resides solely in the universality of the Church, united together by mutual love. And the immutability of dogma, the same as also the purity of rite, is entrusted for guarding not to the hierarchy alone, but also to the whole populace of the Church, which is the Body of Christ".

Khomyakov understood, what decisive significance this formulation of the patriarchs' epistle possesses. Unique in it, after an interval of many centuries, seemingly from the time of the OEcumenical Councils, the Eastern Church precisely and clearly defined its own mystical existence.

And in the depths of Church life this voice of Orthodoxy possessed certainly suchlike tremendous a significance, as did the promulgation of the dogma of infallibility for the Catholic world.

Having perused the epistle of the patriarchs, one is struck in particular somehow by the supra-temporality of it: it was written concerning a notorious and contemporary event and it fully gave answer to it, and together with this precisely such that it might have been written in the V or VI Century, such that its theme manifests supra-temporal truth about the Church.

By such manner within the true Church it is not a church of teachers and their lessons-drills. The truth belongs only to the fullness of the Body of Christ, but its individual members, -- just as for laymen, so also for hierarchs, -- inevitably are able to be mistaken and to sin against the truth.

Comprehending of the existence of the Church is not possible by reason alone. In the preface to the theological writings of Khomyakov, Samarin explains this thus: "I know, I obeyed, I submitted, therefore I do not believe. The Church accepts in its bosom only the free".

The goal of Khomyakov, -- is to reveal from within the essence of the Church. But its authentic essence in definitive form is ineffable. Its chief quality is comprised in that it is a living organism.

By what laws is this living organism directed? What appears to be its fundamental motive principle? What gives life to it?

In the area of the basic religious category of perception it appears to be love. The sole source of the perception and the sole guarantee of religious truth mustneeds be love.

Love by itself defines sobornost'/collectivity; it is unrealisable in individual seclusion and renunciation. But sobornost'/collectivity in turn mustneeds be free. The Church also is freedom in love.

"Every act of believing is an act of freedom and without fail proceeds from a preliminary free searching".

And for this, in order to find the real source of theologicising, it is necessary to assert the integral life of the spirit and to subordinate everything to the religious centre of life.

"The Church is one. The Church, -- this is not a multiplicity of individuals, but an unity of grace, living within the multiplicity of creatures. Only but in regard to human earthly perception does it devolve into the visible and the invisible".

In actual fact the visible Church of living people is situated within the perpetual obschenie/communality with all the Body of Christ and its Head, -- Christ Himself.

Inner sanctity and external immutability are manifest as fundamental signs of the Church.

"By what would the earth be sanctified, -- exclaims Khomyakov, -- if the Church lost its sanctity?"

"The external unity of the Church is revealed in the communality of sacramental mysteries; the inner unity, -- in the unity of the spirit". "Avraam[Abraham] was saved by that Christ, as are we also, -- by the future Redeemer".

"When any of us doth fall, he falleth alone, but alone no one is saved, -- by saving one is saved in the Church".

"Above everything in the Church are love and unity. If they are present, then Divine grace doth accomplish all."

"Ignorance, -- is the inevitable lot of each person in isolation, as also is sin. Only in the soborno-collective of the unity of love is there possible the overcoming of this ignorance".

And from another perspective: "The Spirit of God is not accessed by reason alone, but only by the fullness of the human spirit, under the inspiration of grace."

"The Church in its fullness, as a spiritual organism, is not an assembled substance nor an abstract substance, -- it is the Spirit of God, which knows its very self and is not able not to know."

And actual Church faith, "is a gift of grace and in this time it is an act of freedom." "In the area of faith the world, subjected to the inquiry of man, is not an external world."

"Man finds his own self within the Church, but the self is not in the impotence of his own spiritual solitude, but rather in the power of his own spiritual, sincere unity with his brethren and with his Saviour".

And further: "The Church is the revelation of the Holy Spirit, bestown of the mutual love of Christians". "Its purpose, -- is the salvation of souls and the observance of truths of revealed mysteries in purity".

"The bonds, uniting the earthly Church with the remainder of mankind, are not revealed to us, but we cannot presuppose the harsh judgment of everything dwelling outside the Church."

"Does not Christ love that one who loveth truth? Is not His disciple that one whose heart is opened up to compassion and love? Doth not that one be in imitation of the only Master, perfectly manifesting in Himself love and self-denial, who readily sacrifices happiness and life for brethren?"

"We are free, because that Christ conquered freedom for us by the freedom of His offering of sacrifice." And "whoever doth deny Christian unity, doth slander Christian freedom, since unity, -- is its fruition and its manifestation".

We can attempt to draw a general conclusion from all these definitions of Khomyakov upon the essence of the Church and Church life.

The Church is a living organism, conjoined mutually by free love, comprising an absolute unity in Christ of its members both living and dead.

Each man, living churchly, gains himself its blessed life and organically conjoins himself with it.

The essence of the Church is not exhaustively to be explained by any rational concepts. In order to comprehend it, it is necessary to live in it.

It is life of the integrality of spirit and it envelops existence in all of its manifestations.

8.

Church teaching is disclosed in Holy Scripture and in Holy Tradition. It is necessary to precisely understand what these two sources of its knowledge reveal for the Church, and in what is the difference in attitude towards it between the Western Confessions and Orthodoxy.

"The Spirit of God is manifest in the Church variously: in Scripture, in Tradition and in the doing."

"Individuals do not preserve Tradition and write Scripture, but rather it is the Spirit Divine revealing within them. Scripture, Tradition and deed, -- outside, inside within them, -- it is one only the Spirit of God."

"Every writing, which the Church through the instigation of the Spirit of God accepts as its own, is an Holy Writing/Scripture".

"The difference between Scripture and Tradition consists in this, that Scripture is Tradition written down, and Tradition, -- is living Scripture".

"All the Church in its wholeness has written down the Holy Scriptures, and it gives them life within Holy Tradition."

"And the tendency within Protestantism on the disputed authorship of the Apostles in the Gospel and the Epistles wholly does not alter the attitude of the Church towards them. The important thing is not the author writing them down, but that the Church accepts them as its own."

In essence "within Orthodoxy the Scriptures issue forth from us, -- that is, from the fullness of the Holy and Universal Church, -- and therefore they cannot be taken away from us."

"The Bible is not only a written book, since that what is written, -- is only the visible shell of the Bible. The Bible is a cogitative book, a book as apperceptive source."

9.

It remains for us to make appraisal on the very substantial and complicated question of Khomyakov's teaching.

He speaks in detail about the Church.

But from an Orthodox point of view what indeed for him is shown as the criterion of genuine churchliness? What authority can confirm this authenticity? Where is the guarantee that the Church has not strayed from the Christian pathway, has not ceased already to be of Christ and the one OEcumenical Church?

He speaks in detail about the Church.

On this question, Catholics answer with the dogma about the infallibility of the pope. Protestants seek an answer to it in the free investigation of solitary individuals.

What is the Orthodox answer?

It results from the very nature of the Orthodox understanding of the Church.

"No head of the Church, -- whether spiritual or secular, -- do we accept; Christ is its head and no other do we know."

"The Church is not authority, but truth."

"Infallibility resides solely upon the universality of the Church, bearing it is all the churchly population, -- the genuine Body of Christ."

"Truth is there, where is true sanctity, -- that is, in the integrality of the universal Church."

And the universal Church is more, than even Christ's Apostles, who manifest only part of it.

"Where there is genuine love, freedom, unity in Christ, -- there is the Church."

Even the authority of the OEcumenical Councils is not authority, or in any case it does not manifest itself as authority upon the basis of a juridical legalism of their compilation and work.

A convened council might rightly be perceived by the Church populace as a robber-council, and the solitary voice of a certain ordinary member of it, going contrary to the voices of all -- might in Church consciousness be the unique authentic expression of the voice of the Church.

Thus it was, when Sainted Athanasias the Great, in the modest dignity of deacon withstood the Arian council and personified in himself Church truth. Thus it was also in the time of St. Maximos the Confessor.

By such manner, OEcumenical Councils do not determine the essence of the Church and do nor bear upon themselves without fail Church infallibility.

The authoritativeness of the authentic OEcumenical Councils is determined by that they be freely sanctioned by all the Church populace, under which these sanctions would be stripped of whatever the would-be juridical character.

The final meaning and the final authority lay within the actual Church organism, living the integral life of the spirit. It, -- is free sobornost'/collectivity in love.

From everything said it is clear, how difficult it is for mankind to understand Khomyakov's teaching about the Church, even in regards to contamination by juridical and rationalistic principles.

The expounded core of Khomyakov's teaching, -- with its inevitable terms fashioned by secularised human thought, -- it is necessary to stress, that these terms absolutely do not exhaust the content which Khomyakov encloses within them.

Only to the integral spirit is it readily imbued in the mystery of faith and in the mystery of life.

And although the attainment of this spiritual integrality is very difficult and little to be given one, yet once having attained it, man is able to project out the fundamental spiritual truths of free love and integral life upon all the branches of his thought and will.

Thus also sociability/obschestvennost' is sketched out by Khomyakov, in light of this projection historical questions are also answered, the correct correlation of knowledge and faith is remarked upon, etc.

It is certainly difficult to presuppose that the first attempt in this area would give completely positive results.

And furthermore, the significance of the works of Khomyakov is not to be determined by those concrete conclusions which he draws, but by that for each of his terms, for each expression there sensed his basic wholeness.

Particularly in this chief task, which he set before himself, -- in the area of attainment of an integral view on life, -- he, perhaps, attained to very great and indisputable results.

And yet if one were to seek out the weak side of his philosophy, then by no means is it necessary to do that in this area, but in that there are two diverse measures for the determining of that, to which he is sympathetic and that to which he is not sympathetic.

Thus, having sought to trace the difference between the Western and Eastern religious world, he looks upon the West from the point of view of its empirical imperfection, but towards the East he never even approaches the perspective of the non-embodiment of the ideal by it. In essence by such a different appraising he primarily weakens his own particular positions, which would be more convincing, if he would in both the areas studied speak about one and the same, -- whether about the empirical imperfection in the attainment of the ideal, or about the task, but however not about finding the embodiment of the ideal.

DOSTOEVSKY AND THE PRESENT

by E. Skobtsova

1. DOSTOEVSKY, AS ARTIST
AND PSYCHOLOGIST

Dostoevsky, -- is an entire world. It is difficult to merely even enumerate the themes, which Dostoevsky touched upon in his works. The pathways of the individual human soul and the pathways of all mankind were alike subjects of his profound analysis. The life of a child, -- Iliushechka in "The Brothers Karamazov" or Nellie in "The Humiliated and the Insulted", -- and the ultimate destiny of people, -- the ultimate struggle of good and evil in "The Legend of the Grand Inquisitor", -- were alike attentively scrutinised and inspected by him. As though that children, and the humiliated and insulted people, the lost, the "infernal ones" ardent of heart, -- each individual person, -- a criminal or the elder Zosima, -- by their life opens up and affirms some sort of great truth lodged within them, bearing within themselves the likeness of God, with an unrecurring countenance given by God, in their unrecurrance is the essential and inevitable in the general world order.

This exaltation of the most humiliated and the very least, this discernment in him of the Divine image, -- makes Dostoevsky one of the greatest seers of the human soul and of the human pathway. Without exaggeration it is possible to say, that the appearance of Dostoevsky was a certain boundary limit in the consciousness of people. And all, who now are given to thought after him, might be divided into two groups: the one, -- they that have put to the test his influence upon themselves, they that have passed through the torment and the sorrow, which he uncovers in the world, they are become "Dostoevskian folk". And if they make their way through his thought to the end, then they just as he are able to say: "Through the crucible of doubts my hosanna has passed"... But other people, -- have not tested out the influence of Dostoevsky. Sometimes they too bear their own hosanna. But they bear it the more lightly, since that they do not carry it out through the crucible of doubts. They, -- are always more naive and simple than the people of Dostoevsky, they have not somehow tasted of ultimate mystery in the life of man, and for them it is more easily possible to love man, but it is also more easily possible to fall out of this love.

Dostoevsky was a great Russian national writer. He embodied in his creativity a wisdom unique to the Russian soul; he not only embodied this wisdom, but also revealed to us its content and, perhaps, it is possible to explain much in the destiny of the Russian people, to comprehend and justify much, if it is approached via Dostoevsky. The Russian people is pre-eminently "the man of Dostoevsky". In this is the mystery of its arduous path, in this is the explanation why precisely it was in Russia that Dostoevsky appeared, why precisely he was summoned forth to justify this Russian soul.

How is it possible to define the significance of Dostoevsky? Who was he? Thinker, psychologist, heart-seer, belles-letrist writer, artist? Both the one, and the other, and the third, -- each one. But certainly always the artist. He attains to sublime mastery and artful depiction not only, as customarily conceived, in certain depictions of the characteristics and conduct of people. When alongside the inner content of his narration it becomes necessary for him, he shows us with most convincing clarity also the external world surrounding man.

We remember the first chapter of "The Humiliated and the Insulted", -- cold gloomy Peterburg, Voznesensky [Ascension] Prospekt, old Jeremiah Smith and his dog Azorka. In these several pages Peterburg is thus presented, that involuntarily one wants to compare them with "The Bronze Horseman" of Pushkin. And if we take hold of successive writers, revealing to us the mystery of Peterburg, then in a final reckoning of something new in this mystery, after Dostoevsky they are able to reveal nothing, -- Remizov, Bely, -- they all wrote particularly about the Peterburg mystery, laid bare by Dostoevsky.

And most astonishingly it is, that the world surrounding man, is always presented by Dostoevsky as part of the soul of this man, it is inseparably connected with it, it determines much in it. The external world is posited as it were as an inner landscape of the human soul, it to a large degree determines human actions.

Jeremiah Smith was not able to forgive his daughter not only for psychological reasons, not only since that such were his rules implanted in him from youth, but also from this, -- that it was precisely in this somber and inscrutable, hazy and frosty Peterburg that he lived, and from this, -- that he lived in an attic room resembling a trunk, and from this, -- that Peterburg had consigned him to dismal and melancholy solitude, from this, -- that Peterburg thus particularly perceived became not only the external world of the old man, but also his soul landscape, actualising itself within him and impelling him.

Or we remember the house of Rogozhin in "The Idiot". The very first time, when we read about this dismal house on Gorokhov, we already sense, that it is bound up with some sort of crime present or future; by its somber silence it dooms beforehand the man living in it, to crime, it is one of the accomplices of the transgression.

The park and the pond at Skvoreshnik's were thus beforehand readied for a murder.

Thus it is possible to say: the external world altogether either does not exist in the creative work of Dostoevsky, or not only does it exist, but it also as it were manifests itself as the actualising disposition of soul in the person of its narration, in complicity and in collusion with the person.

Moreover, -- it is possible to track down, that the accomplice of evil and misery, -- of crime, depravity, poverty, -- is almost always the city, -- and the chief instance, the symbol of all cities, -- is Peterburg. It is in the city, -- and invariably in the autumn, -- in the slush and frost, in the wind and rain, -- they suffer, they perish, they sin, deliriously they destroy themselves and the likenesses to them of worn-down and pitiable folk, -- the image and likeness of God.

Truth however and reconciliation, tearful repentance and tender delight usually dwell in the human soul, when part of its inner landscape portrays the earth. It is the early springtime earth by which

Alyosha Karamazov is ecstatically healed, by which Raskol'nikov is healed, the earthy pasted leaves of Ivan, etc.

Suchlike is the external world of Dostoevsky.

But, certainly, his central and ultimate concept is the human soul. And in its depiction Dostoevsky is unequaled in mastery. Intimately and attentively he leads us along the mysterious and tangled paths of mankind, he searches out the hidden causes of human crimes, he explains the strange twistings of soul, he ponders and weights everything, pervasively profound.

The heroes of Dostoevsky are quite varied.

And each of his heroes bears a characteristic mark upon himself at the same time common to them all, -- the mark of "Dostoevskian folk".

It is impossible to think, that people appear in the work of Dostoevsky only to each time enunciate some particular proffering of his philosophic world-outlook. Often he describes for us a character extraneous to any philosophic need for it. He deals thus, for example, in the striking chapter of "The Brothers Karamazov", when Kolya Krasotkin goes to Iliushechka. All his conversation with the market tradespeople, the conversation with the clever yet stupid peasant, the history with the goose, -- all this says of itself therefore, is that Dostoevsky merely is fond of Kolya Krasotkin and desires also that the reader be fond of him in turn.

Suchlike is the small tale of the hundred year old woman in "Diary of a Writer", suchlike are all of the endlessly inserted persons in his novels, -- the believing old women of the starets Zosima, and Jeremiah Smith, etc.

2. DOSTOEVSKY'S MAN

Alongside this there exist a whole host of other figures, -- people, symbolising various philosophic positions. But in spite of this they are all outfitted in flesh and blood, they do not merely think and stand in opposition to each other dialectically, -- they also live, and they suffer and they fall, they repent, they perish, they are saved.

Dostoevsky in a strange way combined within the human soul tenets of very abstract thought together with very real behaviour. Thoughts and ideas themself determine real human fate. Thoughts and ideas become established with obsessive force, they embody themselves, they burrow themselves within materiality, they modify and displace it.

In a majority of instances the major heroes of Dostoevsky are always at root very much centred in themselves. In each of them there is pushed to the limit some particular idea, innate to them, under which it takes hold in clear view apart from the other adjacent ideas, that would balance its ruinous exclusiveness.

As bearers of such ideas appear the three brothers Karamazov, Katerina Ivanovna, Grushen'ka, Smerdyakov, Stavrogin, Shatov, both Verkhovenskys, Kirillov, the lame cripple, Elizaveta Nikolaevna, Versilov, Prince Myshkin, Nastas'ya Philippovna, Aglaya, Raskol'nikov, etc., etc.

N. N. Strakhov says about Dostoevsky: "All his attention was directed at people, and he encompassed only their nature and character. People interested him, people exclusively, with their disposition of soul and the manner of their lives, their feeling and their thoughts." "Neither nature, nor historical commemorations, nor producing works of art were of particular concern to him..."

And N. A. Berdyaev defines thus the approach of Dostoevsky towards mankind: "He takes man set at freedom, emerging from beneathe the law, having escaped from the cosmic order, and he explores his destiny in freedom, he reveals the inevitable results of the ways of freedom."

Actually, Dostoevsky revolts all the time against laws even of beneficial necessity. It was precisely this thought which was raised by the hero of "Notes from the Underground":

"I would not at all be surprised, -- says he, -- if suddenly whether from here or there amidst the future universal happiness would arise some sort of gentleman from the nobility, or better yet to say, with a retrograde and sneering frame, hands derisively at his sides and he says thus to us all:

-- "And why not, gentlemen, to topple over all this happiness at once, underfoot, in the dust, solely for this purpose, so that all these logarithms might be sent off to the devil, and so that again we might survive by our own absurd will?"

"This would be yet nothing, but of course he would find followers. Thus is man designed. And all this for the most empty of reasons, which it seems to mention would not hold up. In particular this, that man always and everywhere, whomever he might be, has loved to do as he wanted, and not at all as his reason and advantage dictate."

"It however is also possible to desire the contrary to one's own advantage, and sometimes one positively must. One's very own willful and free intent, one's very own, and even though it be most wild caprice, it is one's own fancy, though it be at times exasperating even to the point of madness, -- this too is that very elusive, most advantageous advantage, which does not fit under any classification, and from out of which all the systems and theories fly asunder to the devil".

"And why in reality do all these sages think this, that this mustneeds somehow be the norm, somehow this be the voluntary desiring for man? From whence have they assuredly derived this, that prudently-advantageous desiring is a necessity for man? Only the single autonomous desire is necessary for man, whatever the cost and for whatever it might bring.

"There is only one instance, only one, when man can deliberately, consciously wish himself the harmful and absurd, even the most absurd, particularly: so as to have the right to wish for himself even the most absurd and not be duty bound to want only the reasonable. Of course this is most absurd, of course this is sheer caprice, in actual fact, gentlemen, it might be the most advantageous thing of all for our brother of all, that is upon the earth, especially in some instances. And in particular it might be the advantage most advantageous of all in this instance even too, even if it brings us clear harm and were to contradict the very healthy constraints of our reasoning about advantages, since that in each instance there is preserved for us that which is most primary and most precious, i. e. our person-ness and our individuality."

This definition of man about desire was applied towards all the events in the novels of Dostoevsky. His heroes especially are not bound up with prudently-advantageous desire. Essentially, what defines their transgressions, -- is their person-ness and their individuality. And almost all the catastrophes and the disruptions, almost all the failures, and all the ruin, are given definition from within by the willing human person, subject only to it, it is impelled by the principles of its freewill, neither from which are they taken into account nor before which are they diminished.

And indeed for Dostoevsky it is essentially:

"What can be expected of man, of a being bestown with such strange qualities? Man desires the most pernicious nonsense, the most inefficient thoughtlessness, essentially for this reason, to add in his own pernicious fantastic element amidst all this positive prudent reason. He wants for himself to hold on to his own fantastic illusions, to his most trite absurdity, essentially to affirm for himself, that people are all yet people, and not piano keys".

"If ye say, that it is possible also to reduce all this to a formula, and chaos and obscurity and anathemas, -- thus, that given even the unique possibility of the preliminary calculation to remain all that there is ultimately and reason replacing it, then in this instance man would intentionally make himself mad, so that reason should neither possess nor hold sway upon him. I believe in this and answer for this, that the whole seemingly human affair consists actually only in this, that would prove to himself constantly that he is man, and not a pin-nail".

"What indeed would his will here be, when the matter reduces to a formula and to arithmetic, when alone only there is twice two equals four? Twice two would be four even without my will. What would become of his will?

"And is it not therefore perhaps why man so loves destruction and chaos, that he himself instinctively fears to reach his goals and complete the created edifice? And who knows, -- perhaps it is, that everything also which is a purposive end upon the earth, towards which mankind strives, consists but merely in this sole incessant reaching-for? In other words, it is in life itself, and it is not particularly in its purposes, which understandably would be not other than what is twice two is four, which is a formula, and the twice two being four already is not life, gentlemen, but the beginning of death".

"And why art ye so steadfastly, so solemnly convinced, that alone only the normal and the positive, in a word, alone only felicity is advantageous to man? Is not reason mistaken about advantage? Indeed might it be that man loves not only felicity, might it be, that he however loves equally as much the suffering, and passionately so?.. I am convinced, that man under the goad of suffering, which is from destruction and chaos, would never turn himself back. This indeed is of course the primary principle of consciousness".

Here are the laws, to which all the paths of the people of Dostoevsky are subject. All of them strive "to live according to their own absurd will", all of them want not to be piano keys nor pin-nails.

In essence the basic tragedy, manifest as an eternal theme in all the novels of Dostoevsky, is even not so much the tragedy of freedom, as rather the tragedy of human self-will. Human self-will is set by him in opposition to the world order, -- in opposition to the table of logarithms and ultimate purpose, which inevitably equals twice two is four.

And this self-will unrestrained by anything constantly destroys man. Here is Prince Myshkin, childish pure and simple, possessing as it were not even the passion for self-will. But Dostoevsky also puts him outside the laws of necessity, takes him from the general world order, -- and he flings himself about between Agalya and Nastas'ya Philippovna; he is not able to make a final choice, he is not able to decide, since outside his inner stirrings, in the external world there exists no especial reason for a decision.

Another man, unrestrained and passionately self-willed, is Dmitrii Karamazov. He is all the time under the sway of his own self-will. The external world affects him only as a prompting cause for new and newer acts of self-will. So likewise he assumes it, and so he perceives even the beauty of this world setting outside himself.

"Beauty, -- says he to Alyosha, -- is a dreadful and terrible thing. Terrible since it is undefinable, and impossible to define, since God made only riddles. Here the shore has vanished, here everything contrary lives together.

"I cannot bear it, that some man even most excellent in heart and with a lofty mind, should begin with the ideal of the Madonna, and end up with the ideal of the sodomic-pernicious. Even more terrible, that already with the ideal of sodomic-pernition in the soul it does not negate the ideal of the Madonna, but blazes from it in his heart, and in truth, in truth it blazes forth as in the youthful years of innocence.

"Beauty is not the only terrible and mysterious thing. For here the devil doth contend with God and the field of battle, -- is the human heart".

In truth for Dostoevsky it is the human heart, -- this is the eternal field of battle. And there are no sort of powers, which determine who of them will be victorious, -- good or evil, God or the devil.

Man is torn apart by his freedom, and pierced through with the ideal of the Madonna, and tempted by the ideal of sodomic-pernition.

Through the warring powers clashing within him, he is pulled at constantly and self-willedly crosses over from one of them to the other.

Perhaps the most disturbing of all Dostoevsky's heroes, the most burnt-out and desolate, the power of his self-will pushed to its limit, combining in himself the theoretic thought of Ivan Karamazov, -- "everything is permissible", -- with the passionate self-willfulness of Dmitrii, -- is Stavrogin, -- who writes thus is his final letter:

"I tested out my strength everywhere. In tests for itself and for show, it seemed unlimited, just as in all my life before. But for what to put this strength, here I never did see this, nor see it even now. All the same as always before, I can desire to do a good deed, and sense the gratification from this. I tested out great depravity and wasted strength on it, but I neither love nor desired the depravity".

Such are the strange and capricious ways of human freedom, often leading man off into self-will unbounded and even perilous for him.

It is possible thus to say: freedom is absolutely essential to man for his existence. Without freedom he senses himself a piano-key, a pin-nail. In the name of his freedom he sacrifices prudent reason and advantage, he spares nothing neither of such blessings, in order to survive by his own absurd will.

And upon this straight and essentially felicitous path there awaits him the first and terrible temptation. He passes over from freedom into self-will, he is deprived of the capacity of a final choice, and it turns into a playing of contrary forces, contending within him.

This first temptation is defined in the final end by the weakness of desire of the man. If he be not able to desire so powerfully and so passionately the ideal of the Madonna, so that yet nothing except it he desire nor love, then inevitably he begins to be torn apart by the two desires, -- the pernicious sodomic ideal is born in him and rends at him.

And he is hewn apart by ascetic exploit and criminal transgression, betwixt the saintly and the sinner, -- and himself he knows not, what transpires in his soul.

"Such a moment" has come, -- and in "such a moment" -- is the sole cause for his conduct, and he never knows beforehand, what it will be -- this moment.

But this is only the first temptation.

Whoever shows themself sufficiently strong and capable enough for the choice, another temptation lies in wait for them, -- yet the more terrible perhaps.

This temptation is the exclusiveness in the choice.

Many of the heroes of Dostoevsky, having made the choice, having conquered in themselves the tearing apart and being strewn asunder, -- they fall under the power of the choice made by them.

The idea, at which they freely and willingly arrive, which they have accepted through a conscious desire, suddenly begins to twirl around inside just like those dynamic whirlwinds, just like a power, which it is impossible to oppose.

The free man becomes a slave of the idea freely chosen by him. He is as it were obsessed by it. It rules over him absolutely and isolates him not only from the world of facts, from real life, but also from the world of other ideas.

Of the crass, sober, calculating, and essentially idea-less Peter Verkhovensky, -- even of him this obsession is able to manifest an idea, driving him to delirium.

He believed in his tsarevich-Ivan, he does not sense even the alive Stavrogin beyond his domineering idea, which he has fashioned into an abstract grandiose something, to which his self-will has enslaved him.

Or Smerdyakov. Essentially of course the sole reason of the crime committed by him was obsession by the idea, -- "God is not, means everything is permitted". It is only for this, ultimately to embody this idea, to subordinate all his behaviour to it, that he happens upon the murder of Feodor Pavlovich.

Suchlike an obsession impells Raskol'nikov. Everything is sacrificed to it.

And if essentially the suicide of Smerdyakov is explained by this, that having embodied his sole aim in life, -- having dared upon criminal transgression in the name of an idea, -- he does not have further purpose in life, -- then the repentance of Raskol'nikov is to be explained differently: life has spewn him out from beneathe the inconquerable might of the idea. He has been set free from the temptation of obsession.

And here still is an example: Kirillov, having resolved upon suicide, to demonstrate for himself, -- even if not for others, -- the absolute correctness of his idea.

"The man, who resolves to kill himself, for whom it will not matter, -- becomes   god". And in immortality this he does not believe, so that he would then sense himself god for one mere second, -- the second betwixt the embodiment of his idea and death, -- not even a second, but a thousandth interval of a second. But is this not important: the idea, having totally dominated him, mustneeds be embodied, it is not able to be not embodied, he is not able to be freed from this idea, he came to be altogether unable to be freed.

The will to free choice brought him to the slavery of an idea.

From Dostoevsky there is a stunning description of the very process of man falling under the power of an idea:

This is the conversation of Shatov with Stavrogin.

Shatov enthusiastically tells Stavrogin about his faith in the God-bearing aspect of the Russian people.

Stavrogin asks him:

-- Do ye yourself believe in God or not?

-- I believe in Russia, I believe in its Orthodoxy, I believe in the Body of Christ, I believe, that a new advent will be accomplished in Russia.

-- Well, but in God, in God?

-- I... I shall believe in God".

In this short dialogue is shown all the mysterious process, by which man leads himself towards obsession.

In truth, -- the whole overexertion of the will has fundamental significance in it. Choice is made through a passionate force of desire. And this desire hurls itself upon one point, upon one idea. It does not grasp at anything moreso, except this idea.

And here also in the preliminary stage, at which man finds himself, choice for the moment has not arrived. Still does the pernicious sodomic ideal contend against the ideal of the Madonna, and still it is unknown, whether it will bring man out upon the broad road or change upon the thorny foot-path of obsession. It is a stage of investigations.

"Of course the Russian boys how do they manage until now? Some that is? Here for example is a local foul-smelling highway inn, they gather here and crowd in a corner. All their lives before they did not know one another, and when they exit the inn, forty years again they will not know each other. Well and what of it? About what might they argue, while they catch a minute at the inn? About settling of the questions, naught else: does God exist, is there immortality? And those who do not believe in God, -- well, these converse about socialism and anarchism, about the makeover of all mankind into a new state. So this one poor devil departs, all those questions however, only with another ending..."

At this stage it is still very difficult to determine what is the ultimate fate of these "Russian boys". Who of them that might emerge, to conquer the temptations surrounding on every side the path of human freedom, or to be conquered by them, -- to sink into self will or become slavishly subject to some solitary all-victorious and powerful idea.

3. THE MIDDLE WAY

For Dostoevsky, how is the destiny of man sketched out, when left to itself alone?

Here are words of Versilov about this destiny:

"I suggest, my dear, that warfare is already at an end and strife put to sleep. After the curses, the clods of mud and the catcalls, a calmness would ensue and people would be left alone, as they wanted: the great former idea would have abandoned them. The great source of strength, up until that time nourishing and stirring them, is departed, like that grandiose, inviting sun on the picture of Claude Lorrain, but this was already as though the final day of mankind.

"And people suddenly accepted, that they were left altogether alone, and immediately they sensed the enormity of being left orphaned.

"My dear boy, I could never myself imagine people as thankless and stupid. Orphaned mankind would at once throng together to each other all the more closely and the more fondly. They would grasp hands, realising, that now indeed they alone comprise all there is for each other. Disappeared would be the great idea of immortality and they would need to replace it. And all the abundance of the former love for Him, Who was Immortality, would be turned about by them towards nature, to the world, to people, to every blade of grass. They would be in love with both the earth and with life unrestrainedly. And in that measure in which gradually they realised their own transitory and finite existence, it would already be a singularly particular love, would no longer be their former love. They would take notice of such marvels and such mysteries, the like of which they never before imagined, since they would gaze upon nature with other eyes, -- the glance of a lover upon the beloved.

"They would awaken and hasten to embrace one another, in haste to love, realising, that the days are short, that this is all there is, that nothing of them would remain. They would toil each for one another and each would give away to all their means and be happy to do so.

"Each child would know and would sense, that everyone on the earth for them, -- would be as a father or mother.

-- "Let tomorrow be my final day, -- would think each one, gazing at the setting sun, -- but all the same I shall die , yet they will remain, and after them their children.

"And this thought, that they will remain, all so loving and trembling one for another, would replace the thought about meeting beyond the grave.

"Oh, they would hasten to love, in order to blot out the great sadness in their hearts. They would be proud and thoughtful for themselves, but would dispose themselves kindly one towards another: each would tremble for the life and happiness of each. They would become fond one towards another and would not be ashamed of it as now, but would fondle one another like children. In meeting, they would gaze one upon the other with deep and thoughtful glances, and in their glances would be love and sadness"...

Indeed not only, when "warfare is at an end and strife put to sleep", but right now often already these humours are met with in people.

And about what does Dmitrii Karamazov think?

"Why is this there persist the burnt-out mothers, why the destitute people, why this wretched child, why the barren steppe, why do they not hug and kiss, why do they not sing songs of joy, why so blackened from dark misery, why do they not feed the child?.."

In their inner meaning these two fragments are perhaps rather more strange and tragic, than the descriptions of transgression, disintegration, downfall, so often met with in Dostoevsky.

Disintegration, downfall, transgression, -- this is something possible to conceive of like misfortune, it also is not always to be met with among everyone. They, -- are as though it were exceptions from the normal path of life.

These may be the exception generally, -- in every instance it is possible for them to suggest for them the where-abouts of the languishing of a clear and correct life.

Not then in these fragments: in them also is given a norm of life, the inevitable fate of the nature of man.

Nothing, nothing saves him from dark misfortune on nature's paths, nothing is evident on the path of immortality.

What obtains for him before the face of chaos and absurdity, in his impotence and confusion?

Only the single tortuous pity for those like him, the certain pre-death fondness towards each blade of grass. All is transitory, all is non-eternal, all meaninglessly twists round in the world, self-will nowhere succeeds, nowhere takes wing, -- there remains only the pity, only the anguished pity for the lost in the world chaos, in the free spinning of chance for his brother-man.

And this is because, that "without an utmost idea neither man nor nations can exist. And there is but one supreme idea upon the earth, namely, -- about the immortal human soul, -- whereof all the remaining lofty ideas, by which man is able to live, do but flow from it alone".

"Suicide in context of the demise of the idea of immortality reveals itself an absolute and inevitable necessity for each man, who little by little has been lifted up to his level over the bovine".

"The idea of immortality, -- this is life itself, living life, its ultimate formula, the prime source of a true and proper awareness for mankind".

In such manner all human destiny is completely determined by the idea of immortality. Bereft of it, man looses the very meaning of his existence. And each moment of his life he stands as it were on the brink, as it were on the edge of the knife, -- since he has not irrefutable and ultimate proofs of the meaning of life. He needs ever again and anew, and by a most forceful effort of will to believe in this immortality, for otherwise there is the inevitable ruin, chaos, darkness.

"Some quite good man might then suddenly make himself most loathesomely foul and criminal, -- it takes only for him to fall into that delirium, the fatal for us spinning about of convulsive and momentary self-negation and self-destruction, so peculiar to the Russian national character in some fateful moments of its life".

"But on the other hand it is with suchlike an energy that the Russian man would save himself, and usually, it is when he reaches the final limit, that is, when he can go yet nowhere further".

"And it is quite characteristic, that the obverse impulse, the impulse of getting-up and saving-oneself, always occurs more in earnest than the first fit of passion, -- a passionate fit of negation and self-destruction".

We shall have to touch upon Dostoevsky's glance of Russian man in greater detail. Right here it is necessary to trace out in these words the path of the human soul, which always stands afront chaos, which is always able to make itself "most loathesomely foul and criminal", wherein it is predisposed to freedom of doubt and the power of self-will.

But we shall not speak further about things unseemly and criminal. We shall view, whither leads the natural human pathway of man, seeking truth and not desirous of the unseemly and the criminal.

Ivan Karamazov reveals himself as perhaps the most explicit representative of such an ultimately pure human pathway. He knows all the temptations besetting him, he is in the highest degree intellectualised, he argues all his positions to the ultimate conclusion, to the logical end. And even the emotional principle, so indeed peculiar to him, is in essence heated up and determined by his intellect. Thoughts and formulae force him to become agitated and restless. Logical positions lead to practical results.

He is not obsessed by a single idea of some sort, like Kirillov.

Gathered together within him in opposition are all the ideas, which the man is able to encompass, he is obsessed by "human-ness", by the "Euclidian mind" of humanity.

And in him it is possible to study, whither these ideas lead man.

Everything considered and everything apprehended, he arrives at the inference:

"In the final analysis it is the world of this God I do not accept, and even though I know that it exists, I do not indeed entirely concede it. It is not God I do not accept, but rather the world created by Him, this world as being that of God I do not accept and I cannot consent to accept it.

"I have reservations: I am convinced, like a child, that the sufferings will be healed and wiped away, that all the offensive comedy of human contradictions will vanish, like a pitiful mirage, like the horrid contrivance of a feeble and tiny like an atom human Euclidian mind, that at last in the world finale, in the moment of eternal harmony, it would occur and shew of itself that it be then so precious, that it would lay claim to all hearts, to the alleviation of all the outrages, to the redemption of all the misdeeds of mankind, of all the blood spilt by them, it would lay claim, in order perhaps not only so as to forgive, but also to justify everything that has transpired with mankind, -- let all this indeed shew itself, but I then would not accept all this, and I do not want to accept it".

"Not for this however would I suffer, so that by propriety, by my misdeeds and my sufferings, it would fertilise some sort of future harmony.

"If all mustneeds suffer, in order by sufferings to buy the eternal harmony, then why are the children here involved, tell me please? Is it not totally incomprehensible, and for what mustneeds they too suffer, why should the harmony be bought by them with their sufferings? For what then should they hazard into the material and for whom then do they fertilise the future harmony?

"I completely renounce the ultimate harmony. It is not worth one tiny tear though it be only of one deathly-tormented child, which beat itself with little fist upon the breast and pray in a stinking hovel with unredeemed tears to the Infant-God. It is not worth it, because his tears remain unredeemed. They mustneeds be redeemed, otherwise the harmony cannot be".

For Ivan Karamazov here already his hosanna is not able to pass through the crucible of doubts, it does not hold up under these doubts, -- and he would return to God his ticket to the Heavenly Kingdom.

He would accept rebellion and renounce harmony in the name of human chaos, in the name of the unredeemed tears of a child.

In other words, -- he affirms the absurd as meaningful, he renounces the perception of truth.

"Why perceive the devilish good and evil, is it worth it?"

Here is the final frontier for man's pathway. Together with the refusal of good is the refusal of evil. All boundaries are destroyed, everything becomes confused, everything collapses into chaos.

After this "everything is permitted". And together with this the very excesses of boldness, the very great efforts, the voluntarily chosen crimes, -- Smerdyakov, Kirillov, Raskol'nikov, -- in their turn advance no further.

All is permitted, but also all is meaningless. Everything is permitted, since in chaos any grain of sand might arbitrarily choose any direction for its movement, and this chosen direction modifies nothing in the general chaos, it nowhere scrutinises nor organises anything into harmony.

"All is permitted", since no one has powers to alter the offensive primordial comedy of human existence.

Dostoevsky thus by means of the reasonings of Ivan Karamazov brings mankind to the final frontier, resting it upon chaos.

What then? Now, when the mystery of this haughty "all is permitted" is revealed, when it is discovered, that here is manifest only human impotence and disintegration, what then to do for mankind? By what compassion to greet one another? And how to take measure of their everlasting orphaning?

Here only is possible the "to gaze each upon the other with deep and meaningful glances, and in these glances would be love and sadness".

And here afront the face of this chaos, surrounded on all sides by a meaningless and hostile world, having accepted their own particular impotence, having lost faith in any harmony, and having returned their ticket to God, -- mankind can only strive towards its own human unification.

The Grand Inqusitor too knows this. He says:

"Always mankind has striven in its goals to organise itself absolutely world-wide. Many were the great nations and the great histories, but the more advanced these nations were, also the more unhappy they were, since more strongly than others they perceived need of a world-wide unity of mankind.

"The great conquerors, Timur and Ghengis Khan, flew forth like a whirlwind upon the earth, striving to conquer the universe, but also though unconsciously, they displayed that same great need of humanity for world-wide and universal unity".

Earlier on mankind did this unconsciously. Now the veil is removed from the mystery. Left to itself, mankind would realise, that for it there is naught on whom to hope, it would be torn asunder from God, would curse the chaos and absurdity of the world, -- and would strive to rally itself, so that together it would gaze, as the universal sun extinguishes.

In such manner the ultimate conclusion of Dostoevsky about the fate of mankind, left to itself, is very precise: it is not in its powers to bear the curse of its own self-will and it is not in its powers to live in a meaningless universe. It comes to ruin and is permeated by a tortuous pity one for another before the face of this inevitable ruin.

4. THE WAY OF THE INQUISITOR

But in actual fact, in the empirical reality, mankind is not left to itself. There are two forces, which all the time lead the struggle for it, and people have possibility to make a choice between them, to resort to either of them for help.

In the very beginning of contemporary history there occurred the first clash between these two forces.

"Quickly there was perceived the new, previously unheard of until the time of nationhood, -- the all-brotherly, the all-human, in the form of a common universal Church.

"But it was beset by persecution, the ideal was created underground, but over it above-ground was fashioned an enormous edifice, a massive ant-hill, the ancient Roman Empire, likewise also manifest as though it were the ideal and issuing of the moral striving of the ancient world, there appeared the man-god. The Empire embodied itself as a religious idea, bestowing on itself and its issue all the moral striving of the ancient world.

"But the ant-hill did not wall itself in, -- it was undermined by the Church. The collision occurred, the two most contrastingly-opposite ideas, which indeed could only exist on earth: the man-god encountered the God-man. Apollo Belvedere, -- encountered Christ.

"A compromise appeared: the Empire accepted Christianity, and the Church accepted Roman rule and sovereignty.

"A small part of the Church went off into the wilderness and set about to continue the former work".

In this collision of Rome and Christianity there take definition and become commingled the two new forces, which properly define their own path for mankind. For mankind it leads to conflict.

And for Dostoevsky it seems without doubt, that "Rome and its illusion" is the easier for acceptance by an exhausted mankind, and that its temptations hold extraordinarily powerful a sway with human minds. Together with this, -- it is the ultimate path of sinful ruin, of obliteration from mankind of the person, an affirmation of the dominion of the Antichrist, a scorning of the commandments of Christ.

It is here, the final and most terrible temptation, which ambushes mankind in its purpose.

Having exchanged faces and altered appearances over the course of the centuries, this principle antagonistic to Christ remains unchanged in its inner essence. Over the centuries it is guided by this indeed single principle and by the diversity of its faces it conforms itself to the various needs of people.

Dostoevsky defines this temptation most precisely in "The Legend about the Grand Inquisitor", -- perhaps the most gifted of anything he created.

Here face to face he placed the two forces, -- Christ and Antichrist, the Church and Rome.

Rome is not in its ancient aspect, not the Rome of Apollo Belvedere, but rather the Medieval Rome of the Inquisition and "the resplendid autosdafe heretic burnings". But its essence however is this, its eternal immutable essence is in this, that "we are not with Thee, but with him".

And Rome denounces Christ.

Denouncing Christ, it talks about its own pagan, antichristly faith, it talks about what pathways it would steadily lead mankind upon, by what sort of temptations it would tempt with.

Upon the paths of these temptations, "everyone will be happy, -- says the Grand Inquisitor, -- all the millions of people".

"We give them the happiness of the feeble existences, with which they were created".

"We oblige them to work, but in the hours free from toil we structure their lives, as childish play, -- with childish songs, chorus and innocent dancings. Oh, we also absolve for them the sin, -- they are feeble and weak".

"Thou art proud of Thy chosen, but Thou hast only the chosen, whereas we do grant respite to all, and all ours will be happy. We convince them, that only then do they become free, when they relinquish their freedom".

61

Herein is the mystery of the temptation. Freedom, borne by man under his self-will, became for him an already unbearable burden, which is not at all possible to relinquish. The Grand Inquisitor knows this and teaches that freedom is in the relinquishing of it.

"Nothing ever for mankind and for human society was more unendurable than freedom.

"And, dost Thou see the stones in this bare and parched wilderness? Turn them into bread, and for this Thou wilt win over mankind, like an herd, grateful and obedient, though also trembling yet the more.

"Thou didst reject the single absolute banner, which was proffered Thee, which would compel all to bow themselves down before Thee indisputably, -- it was the banner of the bread of the earth, -- and Thou didst reject it in the name of freedom and heavenly bread.

"I tell Thee, that man hath no more tormenting concern, than to find that one, to whom he might the more quickly hand over this gift of freedom, from which this feckless being is born.

"Instead of this, that freedom would be seized away from mankind, Thou didst increase it for him all the more. Or didst Thou forget, that tranquillity, and even death are more dear to man than free choice in the knowledge of good and evil?

"There is nothing more seductive for mankind, than the freedom of his conscience, but also nothing more tormenting. And here instead of firm foundations for the setting to rest of human conscience once and for all, Thou didst seize upon everything, which is extraordinary, conjectural and vague, didst seize upon everything which was beyond the powers of man, and thereupon didst proceed, as though loving them not at all.

"Thou didst not come down from the Cross, since Thou desired not to enslave mankind by the miracle, and didst crave free love and not the miraculous, didst crave free love, and not the servile delights of the constrained before the powerful, having terrified him once and for all.

"But here also Thou didst judge about people too highly, since in the end they are slaves, though even they be made rebels.

"Esteeming man so highly, Thou proceeded as though ceasing to have compassion for him, since Thou wouldst demand much of him. In esteeming him the more, less ought to be demanded of him. It would be closer to being love, since it would lighten his burden.

"He is weak and vile.

"Thou canst with pride point to those children of freedom, to the free love, to their free splendid sacrifice in Thy Name. Yet remember, they were always a mere several thousand, as though gods even then, -- but the rest? And how can the remaining feeble folk be blamed, that they are not able to bear what the mighty can? How can a feeble soul be blamed, that it has not the strength to contain such awesome gifts? Is it possible, hast Thou come indeed forthwith, to the chosen and for the chosen?

"Do we not really love mankind, so very humbly recognising his weaknesses and lovingly lightening his burden?

"Freedom and earthly bread sufficient for everyone, -- is altogether unthinkable, since never, never would they be able to divide it up amongst themselves.

"They are convinced even, that they cannot be free, because they are of limited ability, vicious, insignificant and rebellious.

"Thou didst promise them the heavenly bread. But how can it compare in the eyes of the weak, the eternally vicious and eternally ungrateful human race, -- with earthly bread? And if in the name of heavenly bread there should come following after Thee thousands, tens of thousands, what then should become of the millions and with the tens of thousands of millions of beings, which would be unable to scorn the earthly bread for the heavenly?

"Or dost Thou hold dear only the tens of thousands of the great and strong?

"No, -- for us the ones dear, are the weak.

"In the name of the very bread of the earth there wouldst rise up against Thee the spirit of the earth, and it would contend with and gain victory over Thee, and all would follow after it. Upon the place of Thy temple would be erected a new edifice, there would arise anew the fearsome Babylonian tower of Babel.

"Thou didst desire the free love of man, so that freely he would follow Thee, charmed and captivated by Thee.

"The freedom of their faith would be dearer than anything.

"In place of the firm ancient law, with his free heart man would henceforth need to decide for himself, what is good and what is evil, having in guidance however Thine image before him.

"We shalt have given them a quiet and humble happiness, the happiness of feeble beings, such as they were fashioned. Oh, we shalt have persuaded them in the end not to be proud, since Thou didst exalt them and by this would teach to become proud".

For the Grand Inquisitor it seems beyond doubt, that "it is necessary to withdraw from amongst the proud and twist oneself round towards the meek for the happiness of these meek ones".

And for this there exists a way, shown long ago:

"In the temptations is foretold all the furthermost human history and three manners shewn, in which gather together all the insoluble historical contradictions of human nature upon the earth.

"Thou wouldst have fulfilled everything, that man searches for upon the earth, i.e. -- before whom to bow down in worship, to whom to entrust the conscience, by what manner to unite at last everything into the indisputable, the in-common and harmonious ant-hill, since the demand for universal unification is the third and final-most torment of mankind.

The Inquisitor precisely also to its outcome defined this temptation, by which he wants to lead mankind out from the dead end of self-will and make it subject to him.

Beclouded by self-will, mankind is required to renounce not only it, but together with it authentic freedom also, -- it is required to entrust its conscience to the few chosen ones.

These few, -- they will take upon their shoulders the sins and weaknesses of mankind, and together with this they, -- and solely they alone, -- will be unhappy.

All the masses of the people however, having forsworn freedom, and choice and meaning, would receive the sorrowless happiness of the ant-hill.

In suchlike manner the ideal of forced happiness triumphs in the soul of the Inquisitor over the formerly begun struggle with the voluntary way of Christ.

For even the Inquisitor his way, -- is not the innate and natural way of mankind, -- this rather is the way of the man-god, the way of the few chosen, the way of the faithful servants of the Antichrist, for whom it obtains to conquer natural humanity and close off afront the way to the grace of Christ.

But not only in the Inquisitor, not only in Roman Catholicism does Dostoevsky discern the resurgent idea of ancient Rome and the Roman felicity of the ant-hill.

Here are his thoughts about the French socialism of his time, permeated by ideas of collectivism:

"France also in the Convention of Revolutionaries, and in its atheists, and in its present-time communarists, -- it is all still as though continues to be a Catholic nation completely and entirely, all contagious with the Catholic spirit and its character, proclaiming by the mouths of its very most impudent atheists, -- liberté, fraternité, egalité ou la mort, -- that is, the point exactly is as though the pope himself proclaimed this, it is as though it were merely compulsory to proclaim and formulate -- liberté, egalité, fraternité -- as Catholic, by its style, by its spirit, -- the genuine style and spirit of a medieval pope.

"The at-present French socialism is naught other than merely the most faithful and unswerving continuation of the Catholic idea, its most complete and ultimate conclusion, the fated consequence worked out over the centuries".

"French socialism therefore is naught other than the coerced unification of mankind, an idea, having come from ancient Rome, and then preserved in its entirety in Catholicism".

In suchlike manner the common features amid all the manifestations of the Antichrist idea are considered by Dostoevsky.

It is coerced unification, i.e. the commune (compellere intrare).

In its various features he discerned as basic, -- the principle of coercion. A primary principle antagonistic to Christ, -- this coerciveness is in counterbalance to free choice.

We continue on with the original scheme of Dostoevsky: mankind in its freedom having come to self-will and not knowing how to realise proper choice, not possessing the gift of choice, exhausted by the burden of responsibility and freedom, mankind stands afront the temptation of its coercive transformation into slavery.

"Ou la mort" -- beneathe such a motto it reduces out to universal felicity.

And for the ultimate explication of this way Dostoevsky relates for us the seductive and extreme theory of Shigalev.

The theory is simple:

"The exit out from unbounded freedom I adjudge to be unbounded despotism". -- says Shigalev.

What is this? A social utopia appropriate for all times? A fantastic, semi-scientific project of reconstructing mankind into a new state?

Dostoevsky otherwise defines the significance of such theories:

This "is not merely a labour question, or of the so-called fourth estate, but it is preeminently an atheism question, a question of the contemporary incarnative *embodiment of atheism*, a question of the Babylonian tower of Babel, being constructed without God, not for the reaching of heaven from earth, but for the collapsing of heaven to the earth".

This is extremely peculiar a religion and therefore not at all odd, that "Shigalev looked about such, as though he awaited the destruction of the world, and not at some certain time according to prophecies which might not indeed come to pass, but rather quite definitively, such as on the morning after tomorrow precisely at eleven twenty-five".

Fanatically, Shigalev constructs his system with a purely religious pathos. He reasons out the matter of the Grand Inquisitor to its conclusion. The great equalising -- coercive and with this also salvific -- seems to him the sole solution to the question.

Peter Verkhovensky speaks about his theory:

"To level the mountains, -- is a fine idea, not ludicrous. Education is not necessary, -- enough of science. And without science it would suffice material for a thousand years, but it is necessary to build up obedience.

"The craving of education is an aristocratic craving. Scarcely a bit is there family or love, -- and here already there is the desire for personal property.

"We shall vex to death the desire. We shall allow drunkenness, gossip, denunciation. We shall strangle every genius in infancy. Everything towards the common denominator, complete equality.

"Necessarily only the necessary, -- here is the slogan of all the earthly globe henceforth.

"But convulsings also are necessary. And we as the rulers shall take care of this.

"Total obedience, total impersonality, but once in thirty years Shigalev would allow for a convulsing, and all would begin suddenly to gnash at each other up to a certain point, simply, in order that it not be boring. Tedious boredom is an aristocratic feeling.

"Each would belong to all, and all to each. All would be slaves and in slavery they would be equal.

"The first matter would be to lower the level of education, science and talents. An high level of science and talents allow for merely higher aptitudes. Higher aptitudes are not necessary.

In view of the final resolution of the question, Shigalev proposes "the dividing of mankind into two unequal parts. The one tenth portion would receive freedom of person and unlimited rule over the remaining nine tenths. These latter would need to lose their personal individuality and be transformed into a sort as with an herd, and by unbounded submissive obedience over a series of generations

1

they would attain to the primordial innocence, in a sort as though of the primordial paradise, although otherwise they will also toil".

"Slaves ought to be equal. Without despotism there would yet be neither freedom, nor equality, but in the herd there ought to be equality".

Thus would Shigalev continue on with the idea of the Grand Inquisitor.

Dostoevsky has here indeed many variations. Many perhaps are of various combinations of these fundamental elements.

At the root lies one, -- Dostoevsky is writing about Chernyshevsky!

"You actually would suffer toil, -- not as a bargeman in particular, but so to say as a bargeman in general. To love mankind in general means quite certainly to scorn, and also at times to hate the genuine man standing aside one".

In other words, -- this is a path of surrendering up the human person, a path of betrayal for human freedom.

What seem variations upon this path, are these: on the one side is Verkhovensky and his teaching of honour:

"In essence, our teaching is the negation of honour. And by a candid right to dishonour, it is perhaps all the easier for a Russian man to be caught up behind it.

"The right to dishonour, -- exclaims Stavrogin on this, -- this indeed will hasten all to us, nor would there remain any.

"The very-most chief power, the cement, binding it all together, -- this is the shame of one's opinion. Here thus is the power. And who would this not work upon, who would this not preoccupy dearly, that naught other idea should remain in their head. They have respect for shame".

And here is the other variation, in essence more tragic. The conversation is that of Stavrogin with Kirillov.

Kirillov deliriously affirms:

-- "There will be a new man, happy and proud. For him it will be all the same, -- to live or not to live, -- this will be the new man.

Whoso conquers pain and fear, that one will himself be a god. And this God will not be".

And further on:

-- "God is the pain of the fear of death. Whoso conquers pain and fear, that one becomes himself a god. Then is a new life, then is a new man, all is new. Man would be a god and the physical would be transformed. And the world would be transformed, and actions and thoughts and all sensations would be transformed. Time suddenly would cease and be eternal. The man-god completes the world.

-- "The God-man? -- questions Stavrogin.

-- "The man-god, in this there is a difference, -- answers Kirillov.

Yes, in this there is a difference. In this is the meaning of every temptation. The exit upon the way of the Grand Inquisitor is found, -- this is annihilation.

Dostoevsky particularly analyses out this way to its end. All its possible twistings and swervings, all the temptations met with upon it, -- he pointed out for us.

Here, -- is "the crucible of doubts", through which he carried out his hosanna.

What however is this hosanna? Where indeed is the true and right pathway, set afront mankind?

5. THE CHRISTIAN PATH. TRUE FREEDOM.

The way of ruin, -- is wide. Not only is it wide, but it can tempt man with many separate seductions. Having overcome one suchlike aboriginal temptation, man cannot yet be assured, that he will overcome those following.

The way of salvation is a narrow strait and it is one. It is difficult to distinguish it and to go along upon it.

Dostoevsky certainly knows this and was convinced that he is not mistaken. But together with this, its singularity and sort of non-embodiment in life makes impossible its ultimate definition. During such time as he writes about the ways of temptation with precise words, he presents their definition almost as mathematical formulae, -- the way of salvation is presented by him in a more illusory visage, more rapid in visage of lyrical outpourings, in visage almost of unembodied forms.

And perhaps it would have been yet more difficult and impossible for him to display this way of salvation, if he with his marvelous keenness did not take note of certain almost imperceptible cross-overs between the ways of ruin and of salvation. Beneathe all his acutely negative attitude towards this obsessive possession, which destroys man, he however saw it all wasting away at its base and he expressed it with the words of the elder (starets) Zosima:

"In truth they have more illusory fantasies than have we. They purport to build up justly, but having renounced Christ they will finish up by this, that they will inundate the world with blood, wherein blood crieth out for blood, and he drawing out the sword wilt perish by the sword. If there were not the promise of Christ, then would they so hew one another down to the very last two men upon the earth".

In these words precisely are designated the differences in the two ways, -- the way of ruin and the way of salvation. On the way of ruin are those who, "having renounced Christ, purport to build up justly". Salvation however only is from Christ.

Is this way of ruin final? Is there a turning away from it? Dostoevsky affirms through the lips of the starets Zosima, that despite on the whole its horror, it is not final. The pledge of a return is secreted within the very soul of man, in which truth has not been eradicated!

"Wherefore having repudiated Christianity, and rebelling against it, in actual fact they themselves are yet of that countenance of Christ, and suchlike also wilt remain".

It is necessary to disclose these words until the end, since in their correct understanding is the sole possibility to apprehend, from whence notwithstanding, the hosanna of Dostoevsky is able to proceed through the crucible of trial.

In every temptation, in every fall is something that the human soul undergoes, certain external factours, impelling it towards ruin, extinguishing light and truth from it, but never even to the very moment of destruction, they are never inner elements of the soul, nor something ultimately inseparable from it. The soul always is and remains of the countenance of Christ. Man always is and remains in the image and likeness of God. The rejection and God-blaspheming seem to Dostoevsky as though external garb of the soul, as though constrictively so, through which it passes its life.

No one in the end is cast off, each is able at whatever the moment to recover their sight and turn themselves round, -- each Saul is able to become Paul.

In this belief was expressed the unbounded love of Dostoevsky for mankind. And perhaps all the more tortured and tense he loves a man, it is particularly there, where with an especial force he contemns the temptation, surrounding him about and vanquishing him.

Sometimes he knows even, that peculiarly some sin or vice might reveal to man some portion of truth.

Here for example is an astonishing characteristic of man:

"Here is a very proud man, and many very proud people believe in God, rather especially scorning people. Here the reason is clear: they choose God, so as not to bow themselves down before people, -- to bow down before God is not so offensive".

In these words is the whole concern of Dostoevsky for mankind. He views human vice, -- pride, -- and alongside this he senses the impotence and weakness wasting away the human soul, -- expressed in the need to bow down in worship, -- and finds the way out for it, -- weakness and impotence point to this way out.

Mankind falls away from God, mankind strays away from the true path of salvation, -- how now? Dostoevsky is not outraged?

No, he is not only not outraged, he is impressed rather otherwise:

"This is the marvel, that such a thought, -- a thought about the necessity of God, -- can lie within the head of so wild and wicked a

71

creature as man, to such extent that it can be holy, and affective, and sagacious and obtain honour for man".

Here also much is apparent ultimately: it is both the wild wicked creature, -- and that, which bears the mystery of sagacity and obtaining him honour. The latter always preponderates for Dostoevsky.

And from this perspective he begins to reveal his teaching about the proper pathway of human life.

"Brethren, fear not the sin of mankind, -- says the elder Zosima, -- love man even in his sin, since this be already the likeness of Divine love and is supreme a love upon the earth. Love all the creatures of God, the whole and each grain of sand. Love each leaf, each ray of God. Love the animals, love the plants, love every thing. Thou shouldst love every thing, and thou wilt grasp the mystery of God in things".

Here is raised the solely-authentic banner, -- not the banner of earthly bread, about which the Grand Inquisitor speaks, -- but the banner of all-conquering and all encompassing love, behind which the exhausted and eternally deceived mankind ought in the final end to march.

"Love to throw thyself down upon the earth and kiss it. Kiss the earth incessantly, love insatiably, love all, love everything, seek after this delight and ecstasy".

"Water the earth with the tears of thy joy and love these thy tears.

"Be not ashamed of this ecstasy, value it dearly, since it is a great gift of God, given but to the few and chosen".

And this is not a discourse, not merely a demand of reason, which would find its sole way out from all the doubts and require in the name of its logical constructs an ecstatic love for the earth and mankind. If that were so, then it would be something immaterial, since reason cannot be reduced to love.

No, this is life itself. And here is how this occurs in life:

"The earthly calm as it were poured down from the heavens. The earthly mystery converged from the starry.

"Alyosha stood, looked about and suddenly, as though in collapsing thrust himself down upon the ground. He did not know why he embraced it, he did not ponder any reason for it, since he so irresistibly wanted to kiss it, to kiss it all, -- yet he kissed it, weeping, sobbing and flowing with his tears, and ecstatically he vowed to love it, to love forever and ever.

"And with each instant he sensed clearly, and as though tangibly, how then so soundly and firmly, how this heavenly vault had descended into his soul. Some sort of as it were an idea -- came to reign in his mind. -- and already in all his life and for eternity.

"He fell upon the earth a weak youth, but rose up strong for all his life a fighter, -- and he realised and sensed this suddenly, in this moment of his delight".

It is here, the fiery baptism, by which temptation is vanquished. Here all the human being is as it were transfigured, it merges itself together with all God's creation.

And if the power of temptation weakens one in that it is always on the outside of the human soul, -- then here the power of ecstatic delight is augmented by this, that it is not external for the soul, -- it is its inseparable fate.

Shatov enquires of Stavrogin:

"Did you not tell me, that if it were to be mathematically demonstrated to you, that truth is outside of Christ, then you would be agreeable better to remain with Christ, than with truth?"

What does this mean?

This means, primarily, the spontaneous conjoining of Christ's truth with the human soul is outside the innate power of even mathematical demonstration.

Particularly beneathe all its infinite hardship, this way of salvation is at the same time infinitely simple!

"In Russian Christianity at present it is even also not entirely mysticism, -- in it is the unique love of mankind, the unique image of Christ".

In this is everything. And there is nothing able to withstand this.

73

"What is it in this, that the one has not yet begun to bother itself, but another has already succeeded to get to the locked door and beat its forehead strongly upon it?"

"The same also awaits all in their time, if they enter not upon the salvific path of humble communion with the people".

With the people, -- with the people's faith, -- with the faith of the one only mankind-loving, of the one only image of Christ.

And if man finally finds this saving path, then all his life will be determined by it, -- the relationship to people, the relationship to the world, -- it will determine everything.

Starets Zosima speaks thus about this:

"When he (a monk) perceives however, -- that not only is he worse than all the worldly, but also before all mankind he be guilty for all and for everything, for all the sins of mankind, public and private, -- he then attaineth to the purpose of our unity. Wherefore know ye, beloved, that each single one of us is guilty, for all and for everything undoubtedly upon the earth, not only for the guilt of the world in general, but -- personally, each for all mankind and for every man upon this earth.

"And then only would our heart become tender in a love infinite and universal, not knowing satedness, then would each of us be able by love to reconcile all the world and by our tears to wash away the sins of the world".

Everything is veiled over by love, everything is justified and transfigured by it.

And a sublime image of the joy of Christ's love, its transfigurative power, -- is given in the "Brothers Karamazov" -- in the chapter "Cana of Galilee".

Alyosha falls asleep in the cell of the elder near the coffin. Just then he was undergoing torment by doubt and anxiety, just then he almost lost his faith, he suffered temptation. And he sees a dream-vision:

"He approached towards him, the withered old man with the tiny wrinkles upon the face, smiling joyfully and quietly.

"The coffin was gone and he was in those clothes in which he sat with them the evening before, when the visitors gathered to him. His face was uncovered and his eyes did shine.

"How was this? How did he also happen to be at the banquet-feast, also called to the wedding at Cana of Galilee?

-- "We do drink the new wine, the wine of new and great joy, -- says the elder to Alyosha.

But is it merely and simply a lyrical reflection of the way of Christ that we find in Dostoevsky?

Having worked out so precisely and logically the way of temptation, having put together the intricate and completed system of the Antichrist's pathway, having pointed out the various appearances of this way, -- Rome, the Grand Inquisitor, Shigalev, -- does Dostoevsky give some rather more complete a picture of the triumph of truth, the triumph of the countenance of Christ?

He does, certainly. The truth in it is rather less detailed and it is rather less finished, than those other vignettes. This is possibly to be explained by that good in the world really never has triumphed, and to write about it as embodied, -- is impossible, -- about it is possible only to conjecture, only to have presentiment of it. Evil however is manifold and in various forms has triumphed in the world, and for this, -- to present its image, it suffices merely to look about and write of that, what one sees.

In any case more precise indications about the embodiment of the good of Christ can be found in Dostoevsky. And in the majority of instances its is Father Paisii that speaks about them, -- he that is the friend and follower of Starets Zosima.

Here is one of the most precise of his discourses:

"The Church ought not to turn into the state. That is Rome and its illusion. And on the contrary the state ought to be transformed into the Church, to enter into the extent of the Church and become the Church on earth. This is already completely opposite to ultramontanism and to Rome, and is but the great destined vocation of Orthodoxy upon the earth. This would shine forth from the land of the east."

Here is the opposite position to the forcible coercion of Rome, -- as Dostoevsky understands it, -- it is of the freedom of Christ, of the free unity of love, of the realised Church. This is a final, uniquely-perfect, non self-intentionalised, authentic freedom in Christ, -- the object of the ultimate expectation and hope of mankind.

"So be this, be it, even though at the end of the ages" -- Father Paisii adds, since only in this is the justification of the world and the sole pathway of its salvation.

Suchlike is the general, immutable, and unique resolution of the question.

We shall attempt to find yet more concrete features in this resolution. Dostoevsky has very little of them, -- he not only is stingy with them, but as it were is afraid to be mistaken, and affirms nothing ultimately.

First, what needs to concern us in the searchings of these concrete answers, is the relationship of the truth of Christ to human truth, -- of heavenly bread to earthly bread.

There can be cited here a characteristic excerpt from the conversation of the guests with the monks in the cell of Starets Zosima.

Miusov tells about how some sort of agent of the French police regards the revolutionaries:

"We are not then particularly afraid of all these socialists, anarchists, atheists and revolutionaries. We follow them, and their movements are known to us.

"But there are among them, though but few, very particular people, who are believers in God and are Christians, and at the same time also they are socialists. Here then it is these we are most of all apprehensive of. These are a frightening folk. Christian-socialists are more frightening than atheist-socialists".

Thus thinks a representative of French power, a guardian of the contemporary, -- far distant from being a Christian, -- order of things.

What does Dostoevsky himself think about this?

It is possible to discern his thoughts from out of the remarks of Father Paisii to the discourse of Miusov:

"Do you therefore compare them with us and see us as socialists? -- enquired Father Paisii frankly and without subterfuge".

Here Dostoevsky abruptly cuts short this conversation. Dmitrii Karamazov enters, and the conversation takes on another character.

But the hint is given. Though it be necessary merely to find its corroboration in another place.

6. RUSSIA AND THE RUSSIAN PEOPLE.

Here also arises another essential question. Rome and its illusion is embodied in illustrious peoples, in entire nations, -- the west is imbued with Catholicism, -- even French socialism is the ultimate expression of the expectation of the Grand Inquisitor.

Who is it for Dostoevsky that bears the contrary idea, the idea of the truth of Christ?

How does he approach the people confessing Orthodoxy, to his own Russian people?

No one perhaps has spoken so much about the Russian people, as has Dostoevsky. It is not only from the lips of his heroes, -- Shatov, Versilov, Ivan Karamazov, -- not only by their outlook, -- does he expound his own thoughts about the Russian people, but also in his "Diary of a Writer" he himself as it were affirms the veracity expressed by his heroes.

We begin with the contrast of Europe and Russia.

Here are the words of Versilov:

"They, -- (Europeans), -- are not free, but we are free. Only I alone in Europe with my Russian melancholy then was free.

"I in France am a Frenchman, with the Germans, -- a German, with the ancient Greeks, -- a Greek, -- and by this I am myself most of all a Russian, by this I am myself a genuine Russian and most of all serve Russia, wherein I represent its prime concept.

"Europe however is precious to a Russian, as is Russia also. It is impossible to love Russia more, than I love it. But I never reproached myself for this, that Venice, Rome, Paris, their treasures of science and art, all their history is more dear to me than is Russia. Oh, to Russians dear are these wondrous old stones, these miracles, of God's old world, these splinters of saintly miracles. And even this for us is more dear, than it is for them.

"Russia alone lives not for itself, but for thought. And the remarkable fact is, that here already it is nearly a century, since when Russia lived resolutely not for itself, but simply only for Europe".

And Ivan Karamazov says nearly the same:

"I want to travel to Europe. And I of course know, that I shall journey merely to a cemetery, but to a very dear cemetery, that there one. Dear are those that lay at rest there. Each stone over them speaks about such a fervent elapsed life, about such passionate a faith in their endeavour, in their truth, in their struggle and in their knowledge, that I, -- I know beforehand, -- I shall fall down to the earth and I shall kiss these stones, and I shall weep over them, -- at the same time persuaded in all my heart, that all this is long since a cemetery and nothing more".

And Dostoevsky himself adds on these words of his heroes:

"Europe, -- yes indeed this terrible and holy thing, -- Europe. Oh, do ye know, gentlemen, how dear it is to us, the dreamy-Slavophils, according to you being the detesters of Europe, this very Europe, this land of holy wonders".

In what is the mystery of this attitude to the foreign world, towards foreign culture?

"The capacity for a world-wide responsiveness and fullest trans-embodiment into the genius of foreign nations, a trans-embodiment nearly complete... this capacity is quite Russian national a capacity".

"Our striving towards Europe, even with all its enthusiasms and extremes, was not only legitimate and reasonable in its basis, but also national, -- it coincided entirely with the striving of its own national spirit, -- and in the final end it has also higher purpose.

"The Russian soul, the genius of the Russian people, is perhaps the most of all capable of any nation to accommodate within itself the idea of an all-human unity, of brotherly love".

Suchlike is the tendency of the Russian national soul, -- it strives to manifest itself in the world, in the universe. And Dostoevsky knows, that it strives to manifest itself also in the name of what occurs in the world:

"For the Russian pilgrim-wanderer is necessary particularly a world-wide felicity for him to be at peace, -- he is reconciled to nothing less.

"The significance of Russian man is undoubtedly all-human and universal.

"To become a present-day Russian, to become fully Russian, -- perhaps also but signifies to become the brother of all mankind, all humankind.

From all these excerpts it is already possible to precisely discern certain peculiarities of the Russian national character, which ultimately still define nothing, but in any case, are already indicated. These attributes, -- universality, world-entireness, communality are for all, -- sufferings, expectations and activities of all mankind.

But Dostoevsky takes into account, that "every great people needs to believe, if indeed it wants to long survive, that within it and only within it is that which alone comprises the salvation of the world, that it lives for this, in order to stand at the head of the nations, to unite them all together with itself, and lead them in an harmonious chorus towards an ultimate end, towards all their fore-ordained destiny".

The Russian people fully satisfies these characteristics, -- consequently it is a great people and worthy of a great mission.

What sort is it however, and indeed how does he inwardly define it?

In a somewhat paradoxical form, with a certain exaggeration, -- Shatov speaks about this:

"Do ye know, who in all the world is the sole God-bearing people, coming to renew and to save the world in the name of the new God, and to which only is given the keys of life and new discourse?

"Every people to the present time indeed merely is a people, and while it has its own particular God, it excludes without any reconciliation all the remaining gods in the world.

"If a great people does not believe, that within it is an unique truth, if it does not believe, that it alone has the capacity and is called to resurrect and save all by its truth, it is then immediately transformed into mere ethnographic material rather than a great people.

"But truth is one, and consequently only one of the peoples can have the true God, although the remaining peoples have their own particular and great Gods.

"One people is God-bearing, -- the Russian people".

It is impossible to say, whether Dostoevsky at the end separates these thoughts of Shatov. Briefly, in the given instance, he tests out his own particular thoughts, and reduces them to the paradox of Shatov. In such a form and suchlike exclusivity he does not separate them. But amidst this, his basic attitude towards the Russian people is suchlike as Shatov's.

In "The Diary of a Writer" he speaks much about the Russian people. And here we find, besides a feature somewhat external, -- the proclivity towards the worldwide pilgrim wanderering Russian national soul, -- also its very inner feature, -- that kernel, which it needs to reveal to the world.

"Since the Russian people was itself oppressed and bore its burden of the cross for many centuries, -- it therefore also did not forget its Orthodoxy".

All the destiny of the Russian people is defined by this, since "if a nation will not live by the highest of unselfish ideas, and by the highest aims of service to mankind, but alone serve only their own interests, then undoubtedly these nations will perish, they are done for, they become debilitated and will die".

The Russian nation has this supreme idea. And it is given to it historically:

"The primary school of Christianity, to which the people came, -- of innumerable centuries and endless sufferings, endured by it in its history, when it, abandoned by all, scorned by all, toiling for all and in everything, was left with but Christ the Magister alone, which also it accepted in its soul eternally, and by this saved its soul from hopelessness.

"The Russian people in its vast majority is Orthodox and lives by the idea of Orthodoxy in its fullness, though indeed it does not reason out this idea with answers and science.

"Essentially in our people there is none other except this idea, and indeed everything proceeds from it alone, -- in furthest measure, it our people desires, with all its heart and its deep conviction.

"It desires particularly, that all, who are of it and comprise it, should likewise proceed from this one only idea. And this, despite that it is not from this idea that much of the very selfsame people displays and exits into absurdity, of the stinking, and nasty, criminal, barbaric and sinful.

"But even the selfsame criminal and barbaric, though they sin, all likewise pray to God at the supreme moments of their spiritual life, in order to cut away their sin and stench, and all as it were again comes forth from this their beloved idea.

"And perhaps the chief pre-selective signification of the Russian people in the fates of all mankind consists but in this, to preserve in itself this divine image of Christ in all its purity, and when the time comes, -- to reveal this image to a world having lost its way".

And yet finally one quote about the Russian people, in the end revealing the point of view of Dostoevsky, but producing at first some strange impressions.

"All their profound error is in this, that they do not acknowledge the Church in the Russian people.

"Not for church buildings and not for clergy do I speak now, but for our Russian socialism I speak now, (and I take this contrasting and contra-Church mode of word particularly for the elucidation of my thought, however strange it would appear) -- the purpose and outcome of which is the transnational and universal Church, realised upon the earth, in as much as the earth can contain it.

"I speak for the incessant thirst in the Russian people, the always inherent in it, great, all-common, all the nation, all-brotherly unity in the name of Christ.

"And if there is still not this unity, if still the Church be not realised in full, -- already not in prayer alone and in deed, -- then nonetheless there is the instinct for this Church and the incessant thirst for it, some of the time even almost imperceptible, but it is present in the heart of the many-millions of our people.

"*Not in communism, nor in mechanistic forms* does the socialism of the Russian people consist in. It believes, that it ultimately saves itself only by an all-radiant unity in the name of Christ.

"Here is our Russian socialism".

And here is the clew to the understanding of the earlier cited words of Father Paisii.

It seems, that this is the clew towards an ultimate understanding of the ideal of Dostoevsky himself.

He puts in opposition to all the temptations of the world "the all-radiant unity in the name of Christ" and he believes, that the bearer of this idea, the prophet and herald of it will be the Russian people.

Not very much, it means, did even Shatov distort the genuine thought of Dostoevsky, since he already under his own name purported it in the "Diary of a Writer".

And if one halts especially upon this and says, that with this is finished the foresight of Dostoevsky as regards the destiny of the Russian people, then involuntarily is begotten in the soul a sense of boundless grief.

We know, what we know. Events have brought us to the very final point of disappointment in the Russian people.

"Communism, mechanistic forms", the trampling under of the image of Christ, the coercion of the Grand Inquisitor, the triumph of the thought of Shigalev, of leading mankind from boundless freedom to unbounded despotism, -- here it is realised in fact.

The ideal of Dostoevsky is scorned and despised, his faith was not justified, he did not even himself accept his prophecy.

And there exists the impression, that especially only the negation of his prophecy was justified.

And since he himself with this negative manner contrasted others all the time, such that by these others he enthusiastically said: "this will be, it will be" -- then the one sole conclusion: a bitter sense about the destruction of a great and ardent faith.

The hosanna of Dostoevsky did not know these doubts, -- and if it could know them, then it could not bear them.

7. THE PROPHETIC GIFT OF DOSTOEVSKY.

Is this so? Is it true Dostoevsky did not know these doubts? Did he believe in some then supernatural sanctity of the Russian people? Did he imagine, that thus without a single disruption the Russian people would come to the threshold of the universal Church and lead all the world with it?

For Dostoevsky -- for an expert of the human soul and seer of the heart, knowing all the deep failings and delights of repentance, not ceasing to love man even in his sins, was it odd not to know, that the fate of nations is such as is the fate of individual people --

This surprising phrase is his:

"The Russian people sometimes happens to be terribly implausible".

About this implausibility it is necessary here also to speak.

In what is it?

It is not far to go for examples:

"I think, the quite primary, the quite fundamental need of the Russian people, is a need of suffering, constantly and insatiably, everywhere and in all."

Actually, if this is so, then the Russian people is not terribly implausible.

But a little of this:

"The Russian people as it were takes pleasure in its sufferings.

"If it is able to rise up from its degradation, so then to take revenge for its past falling terribly, even more than it would revenge itself upon others, in formless frenzy its secret torments are from its own particular dissatisfaction".

And this is not only a peculiarity, but is a characteristic common to the Russian people. It is increased by its particular condition at the given moment:

"Yes, it is spiritually sick. Oh, not mortally. The primary, vigourous core of its soul is healthy, but nonetheless the sickness is severe.

"What indeed is it? What is it called?

"This is difficult to express in one word. Perhaps here is how it would be said: the thirst for truth, but unquenchable.

"The people seeks truth and the way out towards it constantly, but does not find it all. With the very liberation from dependence on serfdom, there appeared in the people the need and thirst of something new, already not out of the previous thirst of truth, but already the full truth.

"There appeared then a reckless drunkenness, a drunken sea as it were flooded over Russia, and although it rages even now, but all the same there is a thirst for the new, a new truth, a truth already full, and the people is not lost, drunken even in wine.

"And never perhaps would it be more prone to certain tendencies and influences, and more unprotected from them, than now.

"Take even something from the Stundites and look at its success among the people: what does this witness to? -- the search for truth and anxiety over it".

These words are such, that, when many years will have passed and people begin to study the Russian Revolution from an historical perspective, and turn to the indicators of its origin, of its frames of mind, from which it was created, then as a credible witness it will lead them to the 40 years presaging it.

From Dostoevsky is yet another indicator, also precise.

"They tell about and they publish about the horrors: drunkenness, robbery, drunken children, drunken mothers, cynicism, poverty, impiety, godlessness... If suchlike carousing continues yet though but another 10 years, it will then be impossible to stop the consequences, though it were only from an economic point of view.

"But... at the final moment all the falsehood... will leap forth from the heart of the people and rise up afront it with an unwonted power of accusation. In any event it will save itself, if though indeed it survive until the calamity. It will save itself and us, since again such light and salvation will shine forth below".

Here at first, speaking about the fate of the Russian people, Dostoevsky involves the future time, here he at first speaks not about that which is, but about that which would come.

The time indeed is come, when it mustneeds save and be saved.

It is important in these words of Dostoevsky to understand their true meaning: not from anything of the Stundites, and not from the ease of any sort of influences, not from the drunken sea, -- in a word, not from all the relevant woes contemporary to him does Dostoevsky expect salvation. He speaks all the time about two moments of the future, -- the coming catastrophe and the salvation from it.

And here are extracts, precisely shewing forth these two future events.

"The world will yet save itself after its visitation by an evil spirit. And the evil spirit is nigh: our children, perhaps, will see it".

The first event means -- the visitation of the world by the evil spirit, -- which our children do see. And only second is the salvation of the world.

And here indeed is suchlike precise an indication:

"Actually there perhaps awaits us, i.e. all Russia, cataclysmic and enormous events: great matters can onset suddenly, and take our powers of intelligence by surprise, and then what will happen later?

"Apparently the times have already approached to what then is the centuries eternal, to the millennium, to that which was prepared in the world from the very beginning of its civilisation".

Indeed if people had particularly known how to listen, these words of Dostoevsky would have sounded the alarm in their ears. Now, when we can glance backwards, we sense the dreadful truth though it be of the first half of the prophecy. We know, that the evil spirit has visited the world, we know, that the times are accomplished for the centuries-eternal millennium.

He saw, how this was in preparation. As regards the insignificant signs he drew a conclusion.

"It betakes itself as though a dizziness all over, a sort of itch of depravity. Among the people began an as then unheard of perversion of an idea, in the all-over bowing in worship to materialism".

It seems, that here also it would be more accurate to speak about the future, about this first event, which he anticipated.

In such manner, in very definitive words not able to be ambiguously interpreted, Dostoevsky knew the crucible of doubts, this testing. He anticipated the kingdom and the power of the evil spirit, he did not doubt in its triumph in some unspecified time.

But he saw also the egress from this position, he knew from whence to await salvation.

For those, who would not withstand this temptation and lose faith in the Russian people, his words resound ominously:

"Judge the Russian people not by those nasty things, which it so often does, but by those, great and holy things, by which it even in its meanness constantly longs for".

It longs for and resigns itself to the coming evil spirit, -- the timing means it is still not come, but will come, -- and the people will save itself.

"It is because our people in particular loves truth for the sake of truth, and not for looks. And let it be rough and unseemly, both sinful and unnoticed, -- but come its time and begin the matter if the in-common truth of the people, and you will be amazed at that extent of freedom of spirit, which it will show afront the press of materialism, passion, monetal and property coveting, and even afront the fear of the very most cruel martyr's death".

Nor was anything powerful enough to shake this faith of Dostoevsky in the Russian people. He demands not only this faith, he demands reverence before the Russian people:

"We ought to do reverence before the people and await everything from it, -- both of thought and manner, -- to do reverence before the truth of the people and acknowledge it as truth".

And this is not only ecstatic and blind love for the people. Knowing everything awaiting its downfall, Dostoevsky, as one who is sober and a seer, summons all however to faith in the Russian people.

"With faith in the people and in its strength it is possible we shall yet advance sometime into plenitude and into the full splendour of this our enlightenment in Christ".

Ultimately if these words are accepted, then perhaps here also the thought of Shatov proves itself as then not sufficient, not fully appreciated an idea of the Russian people.

He does not esteem it fully, since not until the end does he believe in God, in the one, universal and world-wide God. With him it is all the time as though the equally-strong gods of the great nations are in competition, and it is only in his basic personal sympathy and love for the Russian people that he bestows pre-eminence to its God. By this he confuses the sequence of valuation. Dostoevsky himself however to the end adheres to the correct and true correlation of values.

For him always and everywhere the countenance of Christ defines everything. All truth is wholly in Him, and evil is not in Him, and is not even for Him in the world.

Here is the key also of his attitude to the Russian people: this people only is great, that it therein bear within itself the truth of Christ.

Therefore, "for mankind a new day begins in the East".

THE WORLD-CONCEPT OF VL. SOLOV'EV

by E. Skobtsova

It is difficult to give an exhaustive account about the world-concept of Solov'ev. It is difficult to combine into a solitary whole all the questions which appear. By its nature the creativity of Solov'ev does not mold itself into a finished and ordered system. Studying it, we have merely various declarations towards various topics, but of a general system of his philosophical world-concept similar to those which German philosophers frequently possess, -- there is not.

The creativity of Solov'ev might be divided into several periods. Prince E. N. Trubetskoy counts three such periods, -- the preparatory, the utopian, and the final. N. A. Berdyaev reckons, that the works of Solov'ev might be divided into two unbroken parts, -- in the first is a majority of his writings, -- it is tinged with a certain extreme enthusiasm with schemes and an absolute faith in the possibility of the embodiment of good upon the earth. The second part, -- the eschatological, -- falls upon the works of the final years of his life. In it the schematicism is powerfully softened and there is no longer the former faith in an indispensible triumph of good. The final victory of the Kingdom of God relates here to supra-historical times. Worldly evil is not victorious at the boundary limit of worldly history. In this final part belong mainly the images of the "Three Conversations" and "The Legend about Antichrist".

The themes which concern Solov'ev in his writings are endlessly varied. Side by side with purely philosophical works we encounter articles of journalism. He writes about worldly history and about the future theocracy, about the poetry of Tiutchev and about the European Question, about positivism and about the Russian Schism, about the OEcumenical Church and about Talmudism.

And when you begin to sort through all this endlessly varied material, there first appears the impulse to distribute it into various compartments, to analyse the creativity of Solov'ev into its component parts, and to address each of them independently, not attempting to find the unity of their source.

But this is only the first impression. Reading the articles of Solov'ev perceptively each time persuades you, that beneathe all the various themes touched upon by them, they have something in common, and this element in common rests in the fundamental postulates of Solov'ev's philosophy, in the fundamental wholeness of his personality, in this, what always and everywhere he by nature seeks after of one thing and then another.

In my task there enters in, -- 1) to indicate what the philosophy of Solov'ev strives after, and 2) how it employs the identified towards the real facts of human history.

I.

Solov'ev was nurtured in his education on Western, German, philosophy. His thought bespeaks the particularly strong influence of Schelling. And having familiarised himself with the great many positings of Western philosophers, he perceived quite acutely the fundamental crisis the West approaches -- a crisis of the general world-apprehension, a sensation of a primordial crumbling, fragmentation and disassociation of the world.

In its essence the Western philosophy contemporary to Solov'ev arrives at a complete negation of the concept of life. In it triumphed pessimism, materialism, and nihilism. And Solov'ev saw a partial truth in many of the statings of these teachings.

But a fundamental attribute of the creative genius of Solov'ev was an aspiration towards the idea of the wholeness of life, an aspiration towards the overcoming of the disintegration of the world. And the question about an authentic concept of life rose up before him not only as purely philosophic question, but also as the immediate practical problem of life. Solov'ev set himself the task of surmounting Western philosophy as the bearer for the crisis of world-apprehension, by means of a synthesis, an unification of everything true that it contains within itself. He attempted to include in his own teaching all the truth, which is encountered in pessimism, materialism and nihilism, even the truth of his own present times' rejection of religion. He seeks after the synthesis, the unification and completion in everything, and his intent is to overcome the crisis of Western philosophy, overcoming the splintering each from the other of theology, metaphysics, and positive science.

In this is comprised the fundamental significance of the philosophy of Solov'ev. He, like no other single philosopher, affixes his own boundary to the history of world philosophy. To a remarkable degree he appears some sort of predecessor of the new epoch. And in this position on crisis is rooted all his error and shortcoming. The philosophy of Solov'ev in many respects shews itself a watershed. After him it is difficult to continue the Western tradition of the XIX Cent., after him the facing up to human knowledge in all its growth makes it a problem to find an unifying principle, and to strive after a synthesis and wholistic world-apprehension.

Solov'ev seeks everywhere universal, not partial truth. In negative teachings themselves he attempts to find the core of religious truth contained in them. Thus for example, the materialist denial of incorporeal truth seems to him a rightful denial of an incomplete truth, which is not able to be embodied. The authentic and complete truth always becomes embodied, always in the end account comes to triumph, always is victorious over everything false or half-false.

From these positions there inevitably results one fundamental feature to all Solov'ev's philosophy: in it properly there remains almost no place for evil, falsehood nor ugliness. For him ugliness is only an incomplete, not embodying itself until the end, beauty; falsehood, -- incomplete truth; and evil, -- incomplete good. In this respect the philosophy of Solov'ev is supremely joyful, supremely optimistic, supremely confident in truth and the Creator and creation, in beauty not only of God, but also of the world and of man.

What is fundamentally the purpose of the philosophic quests of Solov'ev?

He seeks always the absolute or All-Unity, here the authentic reality, which contains in itself all, -- truth, life, beauty. For him the ideal of perception is contained in synthesis, an unification of the whole of knowledge. This wholistic knowledge shews the purpose of theoretic philosophy. According to this, ethics ought to form the ideal of integral life, and aesthetics ought to rework the principle of wholistic creativity.

The philosophy of Solov'ev sets before itself the difficult task to discern in the splintered world-apperception the element of integral, all-unified truth. And the splintering of this tells on everything. Here for example is the antithesis of West and East. Truth is split between them. The West is characterised by a cult of the ungodly man; the East, -- of the unhuman God. And here stands the task to actualise a genuine synthesis, to find the basis for an integral apperception of God-manhood, and not the negative nor human truth of the West, nor the Divine truth of the East.

Or another example, -- abstract principles, manifest as the fundamental theme of Western philosophical speculations. They all, -- having isolated the elements of all-unity, they all bear upon themselves the imprint of the reknown particularism and incompleteness, they -- are not the truth, but only part of the truth. And in order to arrive through them at an understanding of the complete truth, to a comprehension of the Absolute, -- it is necessary to bring them to their fundamental principle, to conjoin into one, to coalesce in the fullness of All-Unity.

By such manner the partial elements of truth ought to fill in one another. There should be found an organic synthesis of the empirical world, of its rationalistic comprehension, and of the mystical or religious significance of the comprehended.

It would be properly correct to say, that the entire philosophy of Solov'ev strives to situate fundamental knowledge and the core of being in a divine origin, and in this divine principle to consolidate all the sides and all the views and the manifestations of worldly life, to think about everything as a single worldly Divine-human process, encompassing within itself all the universe in all its manifestations.

Solov'ev conjoins together into a single creative all-unity -- God and man, spirit and matter, the divine schema about the world together with its embodiment. Nature and human history shew themselves component parts of a single cosmic process, comprising the Divine-human All-Unity.

And this would perhaps explain the dispute that continues to the present day, who was Solov'ev, -- a Catholic or Orthodox, Slavophil or Westerner, conservative or liberal. Beholding everywhere the partial elements of truth and striving to conjoin them into the All-Unity, he was in his work everyman. The quests for universality were by his characteristic nature, quests of the absolute, a yearning to raise up everything relative to a final truth of the absolute and all-one.

II.

Properly speaking, nearly each great work of Solov'ev has for its own basic task the disclosing of the universal all-unity, and the directions of the real paths towards it.

Thus were the "Lectures on God-manhood", such was "History and the Future of Theocracy", likewise "The Justification of the Good". Each theme reveals for itself the pathway from a splintered and scattered empiricism towards a centre of the Absolute. The measure of all-unity, -- is the solitary criterion, by which he arrives at his beloved assertions.

"The Lectures on God-manhood" reveal themselves perhaps most characteristic of all Solov'ev's creative work.

In the first of the twelve lectures, set upon investigating the non-religiosity of contemporary civilisation, Solov'ev uniquely defines its significance: "If Western civilisation possessed its own world significance to accomplish a negative passage from a religious past towards a religious future, then to affirm the foundation for this same religious future is destined for another historical force".

In what here is the concern? Why mustneeds there be a non-religious transition from a religious past to a religious future?

In the Western world the religious past, -- this was Catholicism. It revealed however only one part of universal truth, --

faith in God. And insofar as truth does not suffer detriment in its embodiment, because it must always include in itself perfection, -- therefore detriment always leads to crisis, to catastrophe, to reaction, to negation even of the elements of truth, which already find themselves embodied.

And in reaction to the one-sided revealing of truth in Catholicism there appeared the humanistic period, substantiating the right of human personality.

In particular there occurred the changing of two impaired truths. Catholicism did not admit human truth in the single truth of God-manhood, and by this it determined the tendency in the following humanistic period of history, which influenced everything dedicated particularly to that forgotten part of the religion of God-manhood, impairing itself in the comprehension of the Divine principle.

For this, in order to overcome these dual-sided impairments in the development of the historical process, it is but necessary to conceive the absolute and the divine for human personality. Then in the subsequent historical period, on the basis of faith on God and faith in man, would be realised the all-integral truth of God-manhood.

In other words, -- Western civilisation, having renounced its religious past and the all-wholeness constructed upon the affirmation of human personality, has need merely in the laying down of the religious foundation beneathe its affirmation. And then it actually makes practicable a religious future, because in it there finds their own place both indissoluble parts of God-manhood, -- the principle of the Divine and the principle of the human.

In these assertions Solov'ev introduces into Christianity the element of humanism, and faith in the progress of world history. He enriches religious consciousness with the progressive humanism of a new time. From the other side he clarifies and deepens contemporary consciousness, seeking to ground it upon a firm religious foundation.

Here again there bespeaks his original yearning for an all-unified synthesis.

How did man arrive at the affirmation of the existence of God and the existence of the world? The first act to his affirmations in equal degree appears to be faith in this existence. The very fact of existence of outward reality always yields a non-demonstrable faith, and merely the content of this reality in which man already believed in, is posited by experience. This is applicable equally both for the comprehension of God, and for the comprehension of the world. Man has nothing except faith, no other possibility to affirm the fact of the existence of whatever would be outside himself. But changes to this presumption, we yield to only by faith in the external world; the inter-relatedness of its parts, the relation of it to man is given merely by experience.

By this Solov'ev wants to show that there is no principal difference in the comprehension of God and in the comprehension of the world. If man apart from faith is unable to arrive at an affirmation of the existence of the world, then it is absurd to reject the existence of God only on the basis, that apart from faith it is impossible to arrive at this assertion.

Here before man are two ways out: either he needs completely to renounce faith in the existence of whatever would be apart from himself, or he needs to acknowledge the equal legitimacy both of faith in the existence of God, and likewise of faith in the existence of the external world.

The second act in the comprehension of the world, situated outside of man, reveals itself in his experience. By experience man perceives the attributes of a creature and by experience he perceives the attributes of its Creator. But certainly these differing qualitative experiences have differing content. Together with this both scientific and religious experience in the history of mankind analogously flow in winding about towards a greater depth in the perceived object. Experience obtains with a greater differentiation, the object acquires a greater number of qualities, it becomes enriched and complicated.

Religious experience during the history of mankind has many steps. And the existence of the highest steps of revelation speak not about the non-veracity of the lower, -- it speaks only about their preliminary and inevitable imperfection. The lower religious steps always give merely partial and incomplete accounts about the fullness of truth. Therefore the highest step of religious development ought to be possessed with totality and wholeness, on the other, -- with the limited concrete; it other words, it ought to possess positive universality. By such manner the greatest quantity of positive content defines the absolute religion. Moreover, it is even possible to affirm, that the absolute religion ought to possess all the possible positive content of the world, and that outside it there is no possibility to be any content.

From this it is clear, that the absolute religion is not able to be that religion which is comprised of in all other religions. On the contrary, it ought to comprise in itself all other religions. It is not an abstraction of generic characteristics of other religions, but an unification of their true specific characteristics in the fullness of truth.

Here to a remarkable degree might be brought in an analogy with the domain of scientific experience. In it we have the possibility to observe such development of step-gradation. In it we are thus able to affirm perfection only in the event, if it encompasses for itself everything positive comprising the world. And just as the absolute religion cannot be only the abstraction of all general religious characteristics, so also perfect knowledge cannot unify only these abstract characteristics, but needs to possess full concreteness.

The history of religions provides us the possibility to study the various steps in the revealing of Divinity in the world. At the first stage divine revelation is reserved for the natural world, is conjoined with it, not separate from it, -- this is the stage of natural and immediate revelation.

Further development of the concept about God goes through many phases.

In Buddhism God is manifest as the great Nothing, -- Soloviev terms this a negative revelation and reckons, that by comparison with the immediate revelation of the preceding time, this stage has a positive significance, since it introduces the moment of separation of the Creator from the creation and contributes further to the differentiated knowledge about God.

For the Greeks, -- God, -- everything, -- the universal, is non-differentiated being. Their truth is in this, that as it were they did not devote themselves to matter, creation, and that they attempted, -- true very imperfectly, -- to find out what is this oneness, universality. Their untruth is in this, that for this oneness they completely did not discern person-ness.

Another extreme is disclosed in Judaic monism, where God, -- is pure "I", absolute person, not having that what is set over opposite against the self.

And finally, the completed disclosing of God is in Christianity. Here He is not only One, but also All, -- He is the existing, -- and He is existence.

The partial and incomplete truth of all the preceding religions find their definitive completion and conjoining in the Christian religion of God-manhood.

And prior to Christianity the ancient world came nigh to a correct understanding of God. The Greek philosopher Philo taught about the Logos, and the neo-Platonists about the three hypostases of the Divinity. All the phases of the understanding of God entered into Christianity because the truth in them. But Christianity, being the fullness of truth, disclosed to the world something new. This is that which is signified by the words: "I am the Way, and the Truth, and the Life".

Christianity summoned mankind to a co-operative Divine creativity. It drew mankind nearer to the Divine intent concerning the world. Having manifest as the religion of God-manhood, Christianity indicated the furthest path of development of religious world-apperception.

In this action, -- if the Christian revelation about truth reveals the truth itself and is not able to be supplemented nor unfolded, such that it realises in itself all fullness, -- then from the other side, it however introduces into the Divine arrangement mankind also, with his free will and his free choice, together with all his negative and imperfect world, which not only is able to be discovered and added-onto, but also needs constantly in such the disclosing and drawing-nigh to the divine fullness.

And here Solov'ev expounds one of the most original aspects of his religious philosophy.

God, as Being, as the Logos, as the Word, as the operative Source to bring about all the multiplicity of the world, all its essence, -- is towards oneness. And this multiplicity, having been brought to oneness by the creative act of the Word, is Sophia, the incarnated Wisdom of God. By such manner, the Logos, -- is this existing, and Sophia, -- is the realised idea. And this idea attains its definitive realisation, its sublime perfection only at the moment of co-uniting with the Logos. Sophia, -- ideal incarnation of the Divine idea, and matter having attained perfection, -- in the co-uniting with the Logos, with the Divine Word, -- this is Christ the God-man, by His Divinity, -- the Logos, by His humanity, -- Sophia, the Wisdom of God.

By such manner mankind is shewn as the link, necessarily, whereby becomes possible the unification of the Divine and the natural world. Mankind, once having attained perfection by the flesh of Christ, is the eternal soul of the world, -- Sophia. And the all-human organism, is God's eternal body co-united with the Logos-God in one and inseparable God-manhood. And here the human world soul, the cosmic soul, is first of all co-unified with the Divine Logos in the fullness of God-manhood.

What does this human body of Christ reveal in reality?

In reality it makes manifest the Universal Church, a multiplicity brought into oneness, by a gathering, by a sobornost' of believers, -- or again thus, -- by Sophia.

Here however it is necessary to very strongly stress the relevance of mankind not only to the body of Christ, but also from the other side, -- to the natural-historical world. Mankind with its roots combines itself with the cosmos, and having combined itself with the Logos, it brings all the cosmos to this combining. Whereof Godmanhood, -- this is the utmost fullness, -- in it all the cosmos is divinised and combined with God.

In order to grasp completely this part of the teaching of Solov'ev, it is necessary to show further how he approaches the question about mankind, grasping the idea of mankind in the philosophy of Auguste Comte, -- the founder of positivism.

For Comte humanity is manifest as a living positive unity, a great being, encompassing within itself individual human persons and incarnating itself in the all-world historical process. Just as in geometry the whole at first is of its parts and is presupposed of them, so thus here also the whole of being, -- humanity, -- at first is of the individual human persons and is presupposed of them. From here Comte proceeds to the unique religion of mankind, affirming it as a final concept and final purpose of the world. His positivist teaching acquired a vividly mystical feature.

And disregarding the expressed negation of the Divine found in Comte's teaching, Solov'ev reckoned that many of his affirmations appeared correct even from a Christian point of view. The great being of Comte's religion of humanity appears for Solov'ev as an undisclosed image of Sophia the Wisdom of God, the incarnate idea of God, namely that what in the one God-man Christ is co-united with the eternal Logos God.

The partial truth of Comte for Solov'ev consisted in a correct estimation of the significance and sanctity of the Divine Wisdom. But the falseness of his teaching belies merely the incompleteness of its expression. He honoured Sophia, but the Divine Logos remained foreign to him.

Solov'ev seeks for a proof to his thoughts about Sophia, about its significance in the Orthodox teaching of belief, in a completely different area. He turns to the religious emergence of the Russian nation in the eleventh century. Beyond all the dependence on Byzantium, just merely in the Russian north, they started at this time to construct a cathedral dedicated to Saint Sophia and in it there appeared a mysterious icon: a winged woman sitting upon a throne, and by her sides the Mother of God and John the Baptist, and in front of her Christ and an host of the heavenly powers. This icon, -- the icon of Saint Sophia, the Wisdom of God, -- coinciding neither with the Mother of God nor with Christ, reveals a mysteried knowledge of our ancestors, not encountered in any verbal corpus. They knew the truth of the divinised creature, co-united with the Logos into an unitary God-manhood. Interceding before the winged woman, -- the Mother of God and John the Baptist manifest an image of the utmost summits of creation, true representatives of all mankind, and of all the human one and soborno-catholic church. In particular, they were the chief links hearkening to the co-unification of the Logos and Sophia; they were the summits, from which the descent of the Logos into the world can be associated. And by such manner the winged Sophia conjoined in herself and them so as to take the Logos unto herself, in order that there would be manifest to the world the God-man Christ.

But all what is expressed reveals a fundamental key to the reasoning of Solov'ev. The idea of Sophia and the idea of God-manhood, -- this is what permeates all his quests for the all-unity. All his mystical verses are filled with the mystery about Sophia. In it he seeks after an ultimate unity of the cosmos, and its ultimate justification; in it, -- is the mystery of the universal, needing to be made complete by the mystery of God-manhood.

And here it is necessary further to point out on this, that in the given instance Solov'ev was inspired in this mystery by the pathway spoken about below: initially he believed in it, and then he recognised its content by an experiential pathway, -- the pathway of personal communion, the pathway of personal seeing and feeling.

Now knowing the basic teaching of Solov'ev, it is easy for us to comprehend, what he was opposed to in the contemporary philosophy, and what from it he affirmed as true.

Contemporary philosophy is split primarily between two types: on the one side is mechanistic materialism, annihilating every thought of the world process, and taking away everything in connection with cosmic matter and cosmic force, in which it neither has justification nor substantiation. And from the other side is the contemporary philosophy inevitably resulting in the type of idealist subjectivism, affirming merely the reality of my perceived "I".

That which Solov'ev proposes in contrast to them is a certain religious materialism, the faith in a living soul of matter, -- pan-psychism.

For him man is not only a natural manifestation, nor spirit enveloped in a box of matter. He is spiritual-corporeal, a natural being.

Moreover, animate life is in all nature, separated only in degrees. And if in our own time science does not want to understand this, poetry then at the present time is trustworthy for a correct understanding of the soul of the world. Solov'ev in particular indicated this in an article, dedicated to the poetry of Tiutchev.

What is this? Do there exist in the world two truths in a given instance? No, it is simply that nature for natural science appears merely as an object of study. Natural science does not seek to perceive nature as being. And when Solov'ev, surmounting the generally accepted view, attempts to see in the mechanism of nature its organism, -- then we are able to discern in this the centre of his metaphysics.

Is such an approach legitimate? It seems, that it is not so difficult to argue its legitimacy: it is simple to banish on grounds of insufficiency the purely scientific approach for many of the occurrences in life. Try to analyse in a true sense a work of art, -- how some painting let us say, -- is separated into the component elements of which it is composed. You might precisely determine the composition of the canvas and the composition of the colours, you might consider the combining of various tones and inter-related lines and planes on the picture, but by such manner you would not completely determine its genuine significance, although in essence beyond its veracity, and beyond naturally the plenitude of its scientific veracity, you could say nothing about it.

Nature, like everything genuinely-existing, -- is rooted in God, -- so that it has a supra-temporal and eternal subsistence. Humanity, as an integral universal and individual organism, is world soul. And this world soul, humanity, re-united through Christ with the divine principle, is the Church.

By such manner Solov'ev's faith in humanity, his humanism, -- brought him to faith in God-manhood, and the religious affirmation of matter, his religious materialism, -- brought him to faith in the Mother of God.

III.

A characteristic peculiarity of Solov'ev, his faith in the final triumph of good, his creative optimism he sets forth with particular force in "The Justification of the Good".

But in order to rightly comprehend his optimism, it is necessary to proffer some reservations.

The optimism of Solov'ev is not an assuredness in the good and the blessedness of everything existing, of everything embodied in life. He quickly saw through the shell of incomplete forms embodying the ideal purpose of the Creator. And once having perceived this ideal purpose, he did not want to see or distinguish yet any other. Having seen the purpose of beauty, he ceased to be interested by the ugliness of embodied forms; having grasped the truth, he turned away from falsehood. The optimism of Solov'ev, -- is the optimism of an artist-creator, seeing in the lump of clay the ideal forms of his future creation.

With this point of view the empirical imperfection of the world and the mere potential perfection of the human soul, is merely that system of preliminary material conditions, -- which are necessary for the realisation of the realm of wholeness, -- for the possible embodiment of the Absolute. A chief definitive condition for this appears to be moral freedom, -- the free choice of man.

And here Solov'ev again arrives at one of his beloved ideas, already mentioned.

Since the reality of material and spiritual being is undivided, therefore the process of universal perfection, the future God-manhood, is also God-matterhood.

The process of perfection and approach to the All-Unity, to God, contains with itself all cosmic manifestations, all world history. Outside of this process proper there is no approach to God. And the gradual perfecting, the gradual spiritualising, sets in motion the world.

World history therefore is broken down into five realms, five periods. The mineral realm exists, giving way to the vegetative which, having its own specific characteristics, includes in itself also all the specific characteristics of the preliminary. The animate realm is next in turn, being richer in sense of characteristics than the vegetative, and includes it in itself, so that again likewise it enters partly into the natural-human realm, which was supplanted by the realm of the spiritual-human or Divine. This final realm originates with the birth of the God-man Christ, -- the first and foremost manifestation of the Divine realm.

In the lower animate world the ultimate purpose and the ultimate justification of life serves its procreative endlessness, -- a vicious endlessness, not concerning itself with the individual person and ordering life always upon the spectres of death.

There is a need for man to have some relationship with the concept of life and in some way to seek out its justification. Throughout human history the good has embodied itself. In this is a fundamental metaphysical concept of the essence of history.

It is necessary for man to avoid two temptations, two mutually-inclusive chimera: the chimera of the self-sufficient person and the chimera of impersonal society. For Solov'ev "the anthill of communism and the economic chaos of the bourgeois-philistine realm equally contradict the social idea, such that in the first it abolishes man, and in the second it abolishes mankind". In fact society ought to add to and broaden the human person, and the person ought to add to and broaden society.

Human society passes along three stages of historical development. These stages are the racial, the national-social, and the universal. Christianity, having initiated the universal epoch, does not characterise itself as a negative cosmopolitanism, but is manifest a supra-national and all-national affirmative universalism.

The assertion of their own ultimate ends in the family, in society, and in mankind, correlates to the racial, the national-social, and the spiritual-universal stages.

And our life receives an ultimate moral meaning only when between it and the perfect good there is established a constant perfective connection.

By such manner the core of Solov'ev's creativity shews itself an image of the living, existing, absolute-beauty unity, -- revealed to him in inner experience, in cosmic world processes, and in the history of mankind.

Solov'ev attempts to gather into one positive whole all the created world, to ponder from the point of view of its unity all the processes transpiring in it and in turn not setting it in opposition to God, not separating the creation from the Creator, but rather thus to conjoin in the ultimate All-Unity, in the great Absolute, in the ultimate truth of God-manhood.

An unitary plane of world-creation, rooted in the creative will of the Father and conjoined with it, -- here is what Solov'ev seeks after in his creativity.

IV.

It is still necessary for us to investigate how Solov'ev thinks about the process of world history and how he interprets the whole of individual historical events.

For Solov'ev world history is a lengthy process of the revealing and embodiment of the idea of universal Theocracy. The ultimate task of mankind is the imaging of the Universal Church, -- an all-world organisation of true life. By nature the Church is mankind realising itself, a world soul, Sophia, a worthy co-unification with the Logos in a single God-manhood.

Such is the ultimate concept of the historical process.

And for Solov'ev in this respect the living God is the God of history and not only the One Who is, -- the Existing, but also the One Who shalt be, -- the One to come again. And world history manifests itself as a rational and vivid revealing of Divine truth.

Mankind by itself and the various nations appear as different organs within the whole body of mankind. Only on this pathway is it possible to search out the proposed idea, and only thus does it define the particular meaning of each individual nation.

The single human organism grows. Each historical moment it finds itself set before new tasks.

The pre-christian period, for example, had very complicated and varied tasks. Buddhism liberated the concept of God from the purely natural properties attributed to him. In turn for buddhism, the Hellenic pantheism played also a great role in the approach to true revelation, -- it sanctified matter as a divine principle.

Each nation and each period of history brings mankind towards its final task, -- towards the realisation of the universal Church.

But among the ancient nations the pre-eminent role was played at last by Israel, -- a people chosen by God, potentially including within its own national body all the universal Church.

There are the facts, playing a decisive role in the destiny of the Hebrew people. The first is that Christ by His Mother was Hebrew; in other words, the Logos having become the God-man co-united Himself with the flesh of the Hebrew people. Second, that the majority of His people renounced Him, and it did not recognise in Him the expected Messiah. And finally third, -- that at the present time the centre of the Hebrew people is located in Russia. [ie.1929]

Israel, -- a people God-chosen and God-begetting, -- this is what defines its extraordinary significance.

Finally, at present also the destiny of Israel continues to be exceptionally complicated. Certainly the choosing was never able to be a privilege, but is a difficult and responsible duty. And perhaps this awareness of the difficult responsibility of a God-chosen people explains why the final prayer of Solov'ev before his death was a prayer for the Jews.

At the furthermost, with the Incarnation of Christ, the destiny of mankind assumes a supra-national character. Supra-national is not non-national. For Soloviev the supra-nationality of the Christian period was defined by this, -- that before all mankind was set the task of the Universal Church, in which it was necessary to submerge the national separateness of nations, so as to give way to the supra-national fullness of the universal All-Unity.

But owing to many historical reasons, owing to the imperfection of mankind, -- the one ideal universal Church was split up. And this explains, why the question, which needs resolution at the present historical moment, is the opposition of East and West, having split between themselves the one truth of the Universal Church.

Eastern culture, having subordinated man to supra-human power, is set in opposition to Western culture, the chief principle of which appears to be the self-activation of man.

The synthesis of these two cultures is only possible in Christ the God-man.

"The equilibrium-balance of God-manhood was lodged in the very foundation of the Church. Further on in history this equilibrium was disturbed by mankind on both sides, -- the East, -- on the side of the unshakable divine basis of the Church, -- the West, -- on the side of the human element along both of its polarities, -- at first in the name of power, -- papism, -- then in the name of freedom, -- Protestantism."

The symbolic West and East arose in the opposition of First and Second Rome. Two Romes, -- by nature two parts of the universal Church, Catholic Rome and Orthodox Byzantium. And Western Europe shews itself completely the inheritor of First Rome, having disturbed the equilibrium of God-manhood on the side of its human element.

Russia however, -- is the inheritor of Second Rome, -- Byzantium.

"This second Rome fell, because having accepted in word the idea of the Christian kingdom, but it renounced it in deed, sunken into a continual and systematic contradiction of its own laws and governance from the demands of the supreme moral principle."

And here is Third Rome, -- Russia.

Does there await it to repeat the mistakes of Byzantium? Or ought it to reconcile the two hostile principles, to find the way to a genuine synthesis?

Solov'ev thinks, that "Russia ought to be the third arbitrator in the dispute". This is in other words, -- in taking the unshakable Divine foundation of the Church as it is preserved in the East, Russia ought also to take the human principle, developed into its two forms in the West, -- in the form of power and in the form of freedom.

Russia ought to synthesise them into one Divine-human principle, bequeathed by Christ.

By such manner the Third Rome, in contrast to the First and Second Rome, ought to be a synthesis, ought to be Divine-human Rome.

And so, the contemporary powers acting upon the historical arena are thus: the West, -- inheritor of First Rome, and its religious embodiment Catholicism; the East, -- embodied in the Orthodoxy of Second Rome, having transferred its inheritance to the Third, -- Russia.

Will there be only an opposition of powers, or might the Third Rome, -- Russia, find in itself the courage to be not only the bearer of the tradition of the East, but also the actualiser of a genuine synthesis?

Solov'ev believed in the latter of these, and he reckoned that in a certain sense that Russia mustneeds play a decisive role in the restoration of the one body of God-manhood.

Certain qualities of the Russian people and certain peculiarities of the Russian historical destiny led him to this conclusion.

V.

To understand the inner meaning of Russian history and from the past to derive goals for the future is possible, if one looks carefully at the historical facts.

For Soloviev there exist in Russian history two facts, representing for him national exploits. These were, -- the summoning of the Varangians, and the reform of Peter the Great.

"Russia here was saved from destruction not by national self-conceit, but by national self-renunciation". And in national self-renunciation Soloviev sees in general the primary principle of Russian history.

By such manner the first of these act-exploits, -- the summoning of the Varangians, -- on the one side posits the origin of the Russian sovereign-realm, but on the other side, -- it reveals in this same origin of Russian history its basic principle: Christian humility and the spirit of self-renunciation.

The Russian people, -- is an organic Christian people.

Having accepted Christianity from Byzantium, where it was accepted with formality, where the faith had no influence on life, -- the Russian people in the person of Saint Vladimir knew how to be delivered from this byzantine adherence to Christianity. He understood, that the true faith has the obligation to change the rule of life.

Interesting in this regard is the answer of Vladimir to the Greek bishops, urging him to execute a criminal.

-- I fear the sin, -- he told them.

The principle of Christianity was assimilated by him in spite of byzantine interpretations of this principle.

The Russian primordial Christian inclination towards self-renunciation, expressed in the summoning of the Varangians, combined harmoniously with the acceptance of the faith.

On this true Christian pathway, the first failure and prime temptation was the clash with the Tatars.

"In the Moscow realm attitudes towards the beastly Mongol horde were disastrous. The effect of these relations was harmful in two ways: on the one side the subjection to a lower culture exacted an assimilating influence upon the Russians. On the other side not in that regard, -- the Russians remained a predominantly Christian and historical nation, and this consciousness developed into a national self-conceit".

In the 15th Century this self-conceit strengthened with the collapse of Byzantium and the Mongols.

Liberated from the Mongol Yoke and by such manner having consolidated national self-awareness, Russia with the collapse of Byzantium perceived itself as the legitimate successor of the Eastern Empire, the Third Rome, invested with ecumenico-historical tasks and ecumenico-historical dignity. The combination of this awareness with the legacy of the humiliating Tatar period resulted wherein the Moscow period everything became subordinated to the universal significance of the Moscow state. Christianity lost its universal significance and became merely the religious attribute of Russian nationality. The spiritual strength of the Russian people, having been brought about by the Church, was given over to the strengthening and building up of state autocracy.

As we see below, this did not perplex Solov'ev. He sees in the autocratic, -- if it be genuinely Christian, -- a certain providential significance for Russian history.

It perplexes others.

Here, for example, is the Christian unabashedly monarchist formula of Ivan the Terrible:

-- The land is ruled by the merciful God and by the gracious all-pure Mother of God, and through the prayers of all the saints, and the blessing of our parents, and lastly by us, -- by the sovereigns themselves, -- and not by judges and voevodi-leaders nor even by ipato-consuls nor generals.

But together with this, all the reign of Ivan the Terrible appears as a genuine byzantine contradiction of the wording of the confessed faith and a negation of it in fact. A putrified byzantine pagan tradition overlays the Christian foundation. And this dual-souled tsar affirms the political dual-faith of the Russian nation.

It is characteristic, that during this time in Muscovite Rus', the legend began to spread about the receiving of power by the tsars from Nebuchadnezzar, -- a most typical pagan representative of the deification of principles of state power.

In this legend it tells about how a tsar questions his subjects:

-- Who is it that would bestow to me from the Babylonian kingdom the crown, the sceptre, the hand of power and the book connected with them?

A certain Borma the Wastrel was summoned to do that exploit and he bestowed upon the tsar all the booty. Asking for a reward, he said:

-- Permit me for three years duty-free to drink without paying in all the taverns.

In this legend, as in every exposé of the reign of Ivan the Terrible, it clearly expressed the decline of Russian Third Rome towards those mistakes, defects and crimes, which were ruinous for Second Rome, Byzantium. Under the influence of self-conceit and national exclusiveness, the dual-faith of the Russian nation was strengthened. It obscured its true Christian pathway, founded on self-renunciation. Side by side with the Orthodox Church there was promoted a byzantine-pagan faith in the state and in state power, not connected with the Divine power of Christ.

And then there was a period of a certain equality of state and church power, an equality of tsar and patriarch, -- this was the period of Philaret Nikitich and Nikon. But certainly it is impossible to call this period a time of improvement of the historical error of Muscovite dual-faith.

In particular under Nikon there appeared a tendency towards clericalism, towards the creation of a particular sort of Muscovite papism, an affixing of the church onto the business of state.

And this incorrectly conceived task, -- the befriending of the Kingdom of Caesar by the Church, -- produced two fatal results: On the one side, competing in purely state business, the church power opened itself up to all the secular assaults and it weakened its own purely spiritual essence. By such manner, when this dual-power became inconvenient, the tsar's power shoved aside the power of the patriarch. And it shoved it aside not only from state affairs, but also caused great harm in purely church matters.

The second result of the Nikonian clerical politics was a schism, seeing in Nikon the anti-christ principle and feeding it by the mistakes of its own cultural stagnation.

The judgment upon Nikon reveals all the sins which Russian history accumulated. It indicted Nikon on clericalism, ie. in the appropriating to spiritual authority functions of secular power. But by nature it justified within Byzantium a subordinating of the church to secular power such that, having condemned the schismatics, it turned to the secular power for help against them.

These ascertained and specified processes facilitated the task of Peter, -- the second exploit of self-renunciation, reknown in Russian history.

Solov'ev does not find sufficiently strong enough words to define the significance of the Petrine reform. For him "Peter was an historic co-worker with God, a person truly providential or theocratic". "In his person Russia unmasked the byzantine distortion of Christianity, -- a self-complacent quietism.". "Peter the Great delivered us from the old-believer mandarinism and from the western parody of medieval papism". "The abolition of the patriarchate and the establishment of the synod, -- was the providential wisdom of the reformer".

Together with this, -- and this is stressed above, -- Solov'ev knows, that from the very beginning there was a synod for the Russian Church. He quotes a phrase of Peter about the necessity "to make a spiritual college under the watching from officers of a good man, who would know the synod's work and have boldness". And when he quotes this phrase, he undoubtedly senses its blasphemous meaning.

He writes much and often about the hierarchs, decorated with general-adjutant shoulder-knots and about, that in the orders by the ministry of national enlightenment it is affirmed, that the tsar is the spiritual head of the church, -- caesaropapism, etc.

Such even is his phrase: "At first, before Nikon, -- the spiritual power drew on the sovereign crown, then it forcefully seized upon the sovereign sword, and finally it was compelled to rely upon the sovereign uniform."

And together with this, he believes in the providential act of Peter.

Moreover, -- he says: "This and the liberation of the Christian manifests itself as the fulfillment of certain conditions on the pathway towards the Christian kingdom".

It seems that this contradiction of Solov'ev might be explained under only one assumption: the Russian people, carrying out the mission entrusted to it by God, is not able consciously to carry it out. It was manifest as a blind tool in the hands of Providence. The real demands of life, to which he answered, having completed this or some other act, did not completely co-incide with the ideal tasks of its historical mission.

And thus, -- the summoning of the Varangians, he thought about as a strengthening of the realm, and not about as an accomplishing of the act of self-renunciation.

Committed to the reform of Peter, he strove towards the really necessary for it weapon of European enlightenment, and not towards the ideal purposive act of self-renunciation.

Thus and only thus is it possible to understand Solov'ev, particularly in quoting these following words of his:

"The national question in Russia is a question not about existence, but about the worthiness of existence".

"The supreme ideal of the Russian people, -- Holy Rus', -- excludes all national self-love. For Russia it is always necessary an act of self-renunciation, a spiritual liberation of it".

"Neither did the Normans conquer, nor German craftsmanship swallow up our nationality."

"The spirit, which led our ancestors to the true faith in Byzantium, for the sovereignty principle to the Varangians, for enlightenment to the Germans, -- this spirit always inspired them to search it out not of their own, but of the good".

From these quotes Solov'ev's view on the "journeying" of the Russian people becomes apparent.

In particular also Russia received the faith by way of an act of self-renunciation.

Two other acts of self-renunciation gave Russia first sovereignty, then enlightenment.

And each time, when the Russian spirit fell back from this Christian course of self-renunciation, and returned to this or some other form of paganism, it disclosed a complete failure, it careened off the historical line and did not follow the true path.

Thus it was during the period of self-exalting Muscovite Rus', and so likewise is it even now (in the days of Solov'ev), when hollow patriotism replaces the legitimate needs of nationality, -- as nationalism. All this similarly replaces the concept of the person, -- by egoism.

Now in this false inclination there appear all the sins, that are unique to Russia: Orthodoxy is conceived of as a would-be attribute of the people, state power asserts itself as the head of the Church, and national egoism proclaims itself as the one rational political doctrine.

VI.

Together with this, Solov'ev considers that a national task for Russia does exist and that it is not difficult to comprehend.

"The task is in more direct and universal a service for Christian action, for which both the state and secular enlightenment are only but means. Russia has a religious task in the world".

"For this, in order to understand this task, there is need to leave off from church exclusiveness, there is need for a free and open association with the spiritual powers of the West".

He means here, -- the future salvific act of self-renunciation, -- is a relinquishing of spiritual exclusiveness.

"If we believe in the inner strength of the Eastern Church and we do not suppose, that it should become latinised, then we ought to wish for communion with the West".

"Self-renunciation, -- is an universal, Orthodox matter; we and it, -- are Russian matters. The universal working of God is fully in harmony with the best particularities of the Russian people. And Holy Rus' requires holy work. It, -- is the spiritual reconciliation of East and West in the God-manhood of the one universal Church".

For this, in order to understand this thought it is necessary to realise, that in the God-man Christ are united three services, -- the first-priestly, the royal and the prophetic.

And it is necessary to consider still an other three-oneness, -- the triune Trinity, -- Father, Son and Holy Spirit.

And both the one and the other ought to have an intelligible embodiment in the historical process.

For Solov'ev there are undoubted first-priestly rights, manifest by the Roman throne, -- by the throne of the First-among-apostles Peter, and for him there is an undoubted falling-away of the Eastern Church from that of the Roman, universal, catholic.

The restoration of these first-priestly rights, their recognition, the relinquishing of its own particularity, the entering into of the one catholic Church, -- there is herein an act of renunciation, given us by history.

It is true, together with such a defined position of Solov'ev's query there are encountered words, completely varying all his inner thought.

Thus in one letter to Strossmayer he writes:

"If Russia and slavdom is the new house of David in the Christian world, then surely the divine restorer of the kingdom of David has accepted baptism from John through the tribe of Aaron, the representative of the priesthood".

In this phrase it strongly diminishes the significance of the priesthood of the Roman Catholic Church.

Thus, -- Catholicism embodies the priesthood of the God-man, but the idea of Holy Rus' is manifest as an idea of Orthodox kingdom. The royal service of Christ appears symbolically in the service of the Russian people.

The however prophetic service of Christ requires from history the embodiment of free speech, of free community.

Examining these three corner-stones, -- the first-priestliness of Rome, the Russian Orthodox kingdom and the free community, -- the Triune Father, Son and Holy Spirit, -- Solov'ev proceeds to their conclusions: the Father's power is of the first-priest, the head of the ecumenical church, the pope of Rome, the successor of the apostle Peter. The head of the Christian realm embodies the royal power of the Son, he mustneeds be the spiritual son of the first-hierarch father. And the Holy Spirit must be accepted in the free thought of free society.

Such is the historical task according to Solov'ev.

Here is his exact definition:

"Christian Russia, in imitation to Christ Himself, ought to be subject to the power of the realm, -- the royal power of the Son, -- to the authority of the ecumenical Church, -- to the priesthood of the Father, -- and to proceed off to a suitable place in social freedom, -- to the prophetic working of the Spirit".

It is difficult, and might even be unnecessary, to critique in essence the "Russian Idea" of Solov'ev. In it, as in every purely speculative schema, everything is determined by the task of the author, his need to find answer to the torment of his questions.

For an understanding of his formulations one thing is important: it is important to ascertain the entire meaning of all the world historical process. And secondly, -- to comprehend what in very essence in the tactic of Russian history he accounts as the tactic of self-renunciation, -- that unique salvific leading-away the Russian people from destruction.

But this Christian self-renunciation was an act not of saints nor ascetics, who frequently and on the contrary, were filled with ideas of national exclusiveness and national egoism. It manifests itself as an unconscious act of the people, it sometimes has a sinful and worldly aspect, and it is completely accompanied by rather other occurrences than those, which by nature are implicit to it.

VII.

We have looked at various questions with which Solov'ev concerned himself. We have already noted, that they all interest him chiefly from the point of view of how it might be possible to find in them the way to the all-unity universality. All the world and all history become in the hands of Solov'ev servitors of the final and absolute truth. Everything has its own meaning and its own purpose in the divine architectonics.

And the good, as the final goal of man, the beautiful, as the perfective appearance to which creation ought to strive, the truth, as the ultimate boundary of knowledge, -- all is already set in place in this world and it requires in conclusion but discovery and embodiment.

Nearly all the living creativity of Solov'ev is tinged by a rather untroubled optimism.

In this is perhaps the strength of his geniality, since geniality bears in itself a secret of embodiment and is not troubled by the stagnation of the surrounding world, which in this embodiment surmounts that affected by it. For geniality its creative task seems always already that than the embodiment.

In the formulations of Solov'ev up until the last years of his life there could not be any place for evil, ugliness nor falsehood.

These did not find room in his world-view, and by this is determined the relativeness of their existence.

Evil is unperfected good.

Ugliness, -- is unperfected beauty.

Falsehood, -- is unperfected truth.

The historical process, sometimes having detoured or hindered the legitimate entrance of an event, leads everything towards conclusive embodiment of truth and universal all-unity.

And only in his final years did Solov'ev mark a sharp shift of temperament.

He somehow unexpectedly viewed the real power of evil and falsehood. He suddenly realised, that in particular they shew themselves as the ruling principle of the real world and real history, and that no schematics can swallow up these realities.

Solov'ev became terrified by the authentic tragedy of life and of the empirical impossibility to surmount this tragedy.

But here also he remains true to himself: let evil and death rule in life, -- the creative gaze of Solov'ev turns towards the supra-historical times, and it sought to penetrate into the mystery of the final struggle between good and evil, between Christ and the Anti-Christ.

The most prophetic, most anguished and penetrating thing, that was written by him, was that especially which he wrote under the influence of an impending mental crisis.

This was the Legend about the Anti-Christ.

The world is situated in evil. Evil is triumphant even under the guise of truth and justice. Here is a basic primary theme of the Legend.

The emperor of all the world, the all-powerful master of the world, the creator of a kingdom of justice and outward good, -- he, -- is the beloved son of the prince of darkness, Satan, -- he, -- is the Anti-Christ predicted in the Apocalypse.

In this manner Solov'ev indicates to what degree he has lost faith in the possibility of realising authentic good in the world. The Anti-Christ shifts all the aspirations of mankind over to himself, and ultimately he blocks off the pathway of mankind to God.

But nowhere within the bounds of earthly history is there such a power as can unthrone him. Almost all are seduced by him, and the unseduced, -- a minority of the servants of Christ, -- are vanquished with force by him.

By a magical conjuring of his helper Apollonias the Anti-Christ murders the Starets/Elder Ioann, representative of the Orthodox Church, and Pope Peter II, -- the last Pope of Rome.

There remain but an handful of unseduced Christians be led off into the wilderness after himself by Doctor Ernest Pauli, -- representative of Protestantism.

Solov'ev characterises the Anti-Christ thus: "He believed in the good, in God, in the Messiah, but he loved only himself".

With sinister imagery Solov'ev describes the moment, when at the last OEcumenical Council in Jerusalem, Starets Ioann unmasks the Anti-Christ Emperor:

"Starets Ioann recoiled from him in terror and turning backwards, he cried out in a constrained voice: my children, it is the Anti-Christ".

Then by the magical doings of Apollonias he fell down dead.

The Emperor proposed to the Council to accept a resolution, recognising him as the sole master of the world.

"Suddenly one loud and distinct word rattled through the temple: "Contradictur". "Pope Peter the Second stood up and with a livid face, all trembling with anger, he raised up his stafff towards the direction of the Emperor".

Thus does Solov'ev describe the final days of the world and the final resistance of the Christian Church to the Anti-Christ.

And it is curious that here Solov'ev, saying further that the true representatives of the Church were united in order to resist the Anti-Christ, -- all still he considers, that authentic unification might transpire at the limit of empirical history, after which, "like the heavens sundered by a great lightning-flash from the East to the West, and the faithful beheld Christ, coming unto them in royal attire, with the wounds from the nails on His out-stretched hands".

Here only, during the time of the thousand year reign of the righteous was manifest the possibility of uniting the churches into one ecumenical Church. Here only would Israel finally accept its Messiah.

For Solov'ev "still much would be chattered and fussed about on the scenario, but the drama is long already scripted to the end, and neither spectators nor actors to vary within it".

By such manner Solov'ev, having ceased believing in the possibility of embodiment of the good in empirical history, transfers all his dreams and hopes to the moment, when at the edge of time Christ comes in glory and casts down the power of evil.

The Legend about the Anti-Christ was a decisive moment for Solov'ev's creativity. In the Preface to it he writes: "There is felt the not so very distant image of pallid death, quietly advising not to postpone the printing of this book".

IN SEARCHES OF SYNTHESIS

by E. Skobtsova

(from Journal PUT', no.16, May 1929, pp. 49-68)

Here it is already two thousand years, since the world was assigned the empirically ineffective task, -- to realise within itself God-manhood.

And the two-millennium history of mankind shows this to be an history of empirical impossibility, an history of oblivion, of falling-away, of substitutions, and of impotence to bring itself to the task.

All these failures can be understood only from analysis of the mystical definition of the Church, -- of God-manhood.

Needing to encompass all the fulness of the universe with itself, it manifests two principles for us. The Divine, -- is the principle of Christian Revelation, it implies a known, a given, an absolute truth.

The second principle of God-manhood, -- is the human.

This is an element of eternal developement, of eternal apprehending and disclosing, of eternal perfecting (or conversely, -- of falling-away, of darkening, of failure).

In each epoch there is a maximal point of attainment. Only this supreme tension of human creativity in the present epoch can be regarded as the fullness of the human element. And only in combination with suchlike finality of the epoch can the Divine principle bestow the true fullness of God-manhood.

Just as for the Divine principle from the point of view of the fullness of truth there cannot be two different attitudes, -- it is necessary either to avow it or to fall into the lie of non-avowal, -- so likewise the human principle never and in no wise possesses any firm or precise seal of its appertaining to truth. It is always vulnerable, always open to criticism.

* * *

125

Our times are inclined to declare the yesterday of human creativity a lie. And most subjected to attacks is the very method of human creativity, -- utopianism.

In actual fact, -- over the former ages mankind lived by the flashes of the creative powder-charge of various utopias. It was shoved onto the pathways of history by these utopias. We are indebted to them as real accomplishments, and thus also as downfalls of mankind.

But since this utopianism appears to be one of the most characteristic features in the method of work of mankind, then upon it also is directed all the sharp wit of those who deny its yesterday.

They define utopianism, as faith in the possibility of the Kingdom of God on earth.

We shall try to give this a more formal definition.

Each utopia answers to some sort of pending true need in science, in social life, in philosophy. And always the truth enclosed in it appears in a powerfully exaggerated hypertrophic form.

With this is defined, that for each time period is its own characteristic utopia, -- or its several characteristic utopias.

An utopia manifests itself as a working hypothesis of mankind, facilitating the accounting of accumulated facts, and thus also directing its strivings of will.

And no one utopia, -- working hypothesis, is fruitless in its own time.

It is still possible to affirm, that only maximally hypertrophised and inflated truth impels mankind to intensify its will. This appears as though it were a law of human creativity. Mankind always puts forth its demands for history with the most powerful claim. Having received merely that, which appertains to it in the measure of its historical and cultural stature, it creates a new utopia, manifesting a new claim on history.

Ptolemy, in affirming his system of the universe, thought ultimately, that he was affirming the fullness of empirical truth. It no wise becomes us to say, that his system was only a falsehood, and we are the sooner inclined to assert, that there was a grain of truth contained in it, and it made possible to be accumulated a whole series of factual material, providing the basis of the creation of the Copernican system, which also in its turn was supplanted by Kepler. And the system of Kepler, containing within itself a grain of truth, is perhaps not the final.

Each successive utopia or working hypothesis is related to the preceding, as the system of Kepler was to the system of Copernicus, and as the system of Copernicus was to the system of Ptolemy.

A critical attitude towards a given utopia, and sometimes also towards a very utopian method of creativity, arises then, when the utopia is in this or some other aspect outdated.

It is natural, that some course of events of a successive time might show all the elements of hypertrophy in human creativity. Much is attained, much is swept away. Everything is critically reviewed.

What does this mean?

This means, that the stature of mankind has become higher than the utopias created by it, and mankind needs ... something new, adequate to its growth and its claims of utopia.

* * *

In suchlike manner, knowing this empirically unattainable limit towards which all human creativity strives, -- God-manhood, -- and knowing the methods by which its creativity transpires, -- working hypotheses, utopias, -- it is necessary for us to define that path along which mankind went in preceding eras of its developement.

Historical practice, certainly, in no one stage of its developement can provide us full proximity to a combination of the two principles, -- the Divine and the human.

Only the first centuries of Christianity, -- the period of the Church Councils, -- to a certain degree justify the theory. The human principle in the Church, in God-manhood, -- was then presented in it maximal creative completeness. The Greek culture and philosophy nurturing Byzantium is wholly and inseparably bound up with this initial period of the history of the Church. More intense and vast a discourse mankind did not then create.

And this discourse was combined with the proclaiming of Revelation, creating an unity in-common, approximating to an embodiment of God-manhood.

It was perhaps the period of Athanasias the Great, -- a period of harmonic combination of divine Revelation and human wisdom, -- that in truth was the golden age of Christian mankind.

It is characteristic, that even in this golden age it is possible to find an authentic human utopia.

Constantine the Great can be reckoned the creator of this utopia.

In the Divine Revelation it was fore-ordained for him to conquer by the cross.

His human inclination towards utopianism substituted the cross by a sword, it sanctified the sword.

Now, after many centuries it mustneeds be said, that in this working hypothesis of defining directions of human creativity, there was quite certainly an element of this indeed hypertrophy of truth. A positive feature was affirmed in society -- state-building. This creativity was introduced into the system of humanly sanctioned creativity.

A blow was inflicted by this upon the idea of the beastly-wild nature of the civil society, and there was laid a foundation for penetration of Christianity into this part of human creativity.

After the period of the first centuries of Christianity, there began in the Church a process of slow ossification, -- of a gradual transition into a static condition of the human dynamic principle.

The attributes of the Divine principle, -- fullness bestown by Revelation, -- were gradually transferred once for all to the fixed moment of the creative tension of mankind.

In their reverence afront the given for a certain moment of fullness of God-manhood, people as it were caught up in their element, entering into this fullness, with the properties of motionless Divine truth.

Beneathe this standard stood all the medieval period of history.

If philosophy stopped with Aristotle, and if the system of Ptolemy were the final one, and if Church consciousness were static, then further than this mankind should not make bold to dare.

In this was the one-sidedness of the Middle Ages, its abdication from the human principle.

The stasis of human creativity became imponderable.

The idea of God-manhood withered and was swallowed up.

Finally, in the balance-swinging to this unhealthy process, lasting whole centuries, mankind began gradually to emerge from this diminished church. The ossified church as it were no longer covered all mankind with its cupola, and gradually almost everything creative sensed itself not beneathe this cupola, but beneathe the open sky, -- it sensed itself with a different array of responsibility, a different tension of freedom, with a different direction of creative yearning.

In actual fact, when it occurred to Copernicus, -- in contrast to the position of the church -- to assert the movement of the earth around the sun, when man sensed, that before him, on the one side was the authority of the Church and the necessity to deny the fact, grasped and affirmed by his creative intensity, and on the other, -- the bon-fire of the Inquisition indeed a fact, which he could not deny, -- therein all the stability of the Middle Ages was shaken asunder.

The empirical church, as it were, consigned to the grave the idea of God-manhood, it shoved mankind out upon the wide highway of the world, directing him not by revelations, but rather by natural laws.

What was mankind to do?

It had to go and it went by another way.

These pathways led off away from the Church. Afront mankind there was opened up an epoch of great attainments and discoveries, an epoch of the blossoming of all the human spiritual and creative powers.

And that human element, which was fixedly set within the church, could not compare with the new attainments.

But even on its part humanism was not anti-God, -- it was merely godless. And this godlessness was not primarily expounded by humanism, it appeared only in reaction to the inhumanity of the preceding period.

The many centuries of creative prohibition resulted in the tempestuous creative Renaissance. All the dynamism of human nature was embodied in life. And the world occupied itself with the construction of its worldly affairs.

Ultimately, this process was in essence also an one-sided process. God-manhood abdicated its Divine nature, it affirmed only the human and by this overshot the mark to the other side.

But just as the Middle Ages in the area of approach to God was intense and filled with values, so also humanism, -- the new history, -- in full measure disclosed and cultivated the value of the human person, it rightly defined it upon freedom and intensified its creative possibilities.

For the empirical Church there remained only its unique entree, the preservation of Divine truth.

In such manner mankind was inwardly emancipated, having affirmed its right to free creativity.

And here, upon these purely human pathways, deprived of the Divine principle of the Church, in the utopias continuously being created and replacing one another, there began to issue forth a certain surrogate to substitute for the religious principle.

In such manner, the reverse process had parallels with all the elements that had begotten it.

Now it is possible to assert, that inwardly the vast way-station is gone by. Mankind has struck the creative spark, lodged within it at the present time. Mankind enmasse is satiated with creativity and outgrows itself.

The created utopias at this or some other step have added in the seed of their embodied truth into the common treasury of mankind, and in the aspect of their hypertrophy they have ceased to captivate or stimulate mankind.

And now we stand afront tormenting searches for new ways.

The contemporary world cannot continue to work and to create by the old methods of creation of winged utopias.

For this some sort of new premises are needed. For this the very basics of creativity mustneeds be re-examined.

All the multi-valued harvest of humanism is gathered and packed up in the storehouse of human culture.

*   *   *

In the history of Russian culture we can recognise all the elements, that defined Western culture. Only the manner of their combination and disclosing was different.

Whereas in the West ideas had a prolonged period of growth and maturation, and slowly conquered life, -- in the history of Russian culture ideas appeared by the revolutionary pathway, -- they were introduced in readied form and almost forcibly engrafted onto Russian culture.

Russian culture was always fractured and shredded, and then came down to its full form, to the endpoint of each idea.

Everything was reduced to its endpoint.

For Russian culture the Baptism of Rus' in the waters of the Dniepr was characteristic.

Revolutionary, like a lightning-flash, almost without a period of previous maturation, Christianity was bestown upon ancient Rus'. It was not bestown as a gradual preparation of minds, not as a whole series of preparatory decades, but rather all in full, -- complete.

The pagan gods did not retreat slowly before the conquering cross, but rather Perun was cast down in all his almightiness. It was no sort "an altar to the unknown God" that then was dispatched in this. The blow to Perun was struck without warning and straight to the head.

And upon Rus' there burned not only a light, but a veritable blazing with Christianity.

The Russian cultural legacy of Byzantium was carried over through Kievan Rus' into Muscovite Rus', having passed through the straits of the Tatar-Mongol Yoke.

And this legacy was appropriated not in some partial aspect, but all entirely.

Orthodoxy in entirety defined Russian spiritual culture.

And the secular, human concepts of Byzantium, the utopia of Constantine the Great, substituting the sword for the cross, defined the consciousness of Muscovite Rus'.

-- Moscow, -- the Third Rome. A fourth there would not be. --

Here it is, one of the first Russian utopias, fluttering about and fanning the consciousness of Muscovite man.

And in it there was, certainly, a grain of truth. It defined for itself the tenacious, cohesive and passionate amassing of the great realm. It synthesised bringing together within itself over the long centuries all the separate responses to Russian culture, it absorbed and assimilated the Tatar period, it set itself in opposition to East and to West, -- in a word, -- it interlaced and nurtured the Russian culture.

Russian spiritual and secular culture possessed during this period a certain single mystical visage. And if an apocalypse were to be written at the time, then in the Russian Church they would give an accounting to the angel, for merit and for fault, for all the merits and faults of Russian culture in synthesis and conjoined by Orthodoxy.

And so Russian history in this regard went somewhat a different path.

During this period, which we can term the Russian Middle Ages, there were not the features characteristic to the West. The human principle did not sense itself crowded beneathe the church cupola. The empirical Orthodox Church did not set up the Divine principle in opposition, as a Revelation rigid and given once for always, -- in opposition to the fluid course of human creativity.

And if historically it is possible to say, that all the reforms of Peter were defined and prepared for by the preceding period, then in saying this, then it is sooner necessary to consider not the culture in the narrow sense of the word, but rather and chiefly to compare the uneven growth of external Russian civilisation in comparison with the civilisation of the West.

In the area of culture the reform of Peter was revolutionary, inwardly it was not readied, not connected organically with the Russian yesterday.

They shaved the boyars of their beards and crammed them into European waistjackets with coat-tails, -- possibly if so to speak, -- without any inner basis for it. Although the external reasons were quite sufficient.

Peter toppled the preceding Russian culture and dragged it to its ruin by suchlike similar a revolutionary act, as in his own time Vladimir dragged Perun into the waters of the Dniepr.

Revolutionary, lightning-like and contagiously, on the model of Western culture, the human element was chopped off from the Church.

Pathways outside the Church were pointed out for human creativity.

And in order that nothing might shove the history of secular culture backwards, -- beneathe the Church cupola, -- the Church was deprived of all signs of external connection with the world, it was decapitated, even in its organisation it was made subject to the state, -- there remained for it only a single branch of creativity, -- it could concern itself but with the salvation of souls, manifest as proper to the most intimate life of man, while not permeating the whole of him with its majestic truth.

Thus the revolutionary Russian culture was split and splintered.

We see, that all the eighteenth century of Russian culture, which seems to us artificial and inorganic, -- was completely unaffected by religious questions. They built universities, they opened the Academy, and they write about the utility of glass, they study Europe, they imitate it, they have tsars of stern German stock and soldier uniforms of the Prussian fashion, and a court with the pomp surpassing Versailles, and mannerisms of pre Revolutionary France, and quick growth of external majesty, and Lomonosov, and Fon-Vizin, -- but no wise and nowhere heard a single word, laying a bridge between the secular and church cultures.

And during this period however were hid in the forests the schismatic Raskolniki, partisans of the old faith, during this time in the desolate monasteries ascetics save themselves, -- the spiritual deed of salvation of souls and the increase of the flock of Christ takes place somewhere out of sight, little connected with the mostholy governing synod, and with all the resplendid external decoration of the Church, the necessity for official moliebens in prayer for "the Most-Pious, the Most-Autocratic", and still moreso necessary, in order on the example of Byzantium by means of chrism-anointing to conjoin for "the Most-Pious and Most-Autocratic" not only the might of a worldly ruler, but also the majesty of being the Lord's chosen.

Thus was accomplished a most grand and most tragic schism and split in the unique visage of Russian culture.

Who now at present can themself really imagine, that St. Seraphim of Sarov and Pushkin were contemporaries? Really does it not seem for us, -- essentially indeed, -- that they lived on different planets?

St. Seraphim of Sarov, Optina Pustyn' and much, much else, -- the thread of spiritual culture is not broken, it stands contrary to synodal politics, -- inwardly it surmounts it. Beneathe the bushel-basket shines the Church light. All this light of it belongs entirely to the same Russian culture, but the paths for touching between its two channels are done with.

Mankind however, the purely human creativity goes by another path, the godless way.

The Church is fenced off from human creativity by its own official and moribund, or by its never formerly alive (like the synod) encasings.

To mankind was granted only to create utopias or become infected by foreign utopias; to appropriate their winged, hypertrophic aspect as a certain surrogate for religion.

Almost all the truly-creative thoughts of the Russian Intelligentsia were suchlike surrogates for religion, or else a vague and hopeless thirst for this religious principle.

The Russian Intelligentsia managed from its most staid, its most insipid and dull teaching, from its least winged utopia, -- Marxism, -- to create occasion for basic religious survival and for religious martyrdom.

Certainly in the history of the XIX Century immense significance is had by those creators of Russian culture, who foresaw its somehow inevitable unity, and who, being genuine geniuses of human thought, united themselves together with the church holy things.

Yet in essence it is not only such Christians as Kireevsky, Khomyakov, Samarin, Dostoevsky, Solov'ev, and moreso later, -- but also the positivist Hertsen in equal degree; they all define Russian culture.

And just as the figure of Hertsen wanting for synthesis choiced upon this impossibility in synthesis to substantiate and justify human pathways, -- so also in equal measure, having discovered for himself personally the synthesis of God-manhood, Dostoevsky was a figure genuinely tragic, since the individual synthesis could not cover over the abyss of the schism, but merely fractured man eternally betwixt the two shores.

With this, all who personally were in synthesis, who comprehended in secret the embodiment of God-manhood, appeared merely as remote prophets of a new era, and for their own time they resounded not fully. Their contemporaries always considered them impaired, excusing them because of their genius or talent, -- the one, -- a resident on the shore of spiritual culture, -- the other, -- a communicant of secular culture.

In such manner, perhaps not so organically as in Europe, not so by measure of law and gradually, but in essence with great morbid complications, with great moral impasses, God-manhood was crucified for us in Russia. Its single visage seemed split. Two worlds lived side by side, not touching.

*   *   *

Finally the sum total. The present day. Bol'shevism ...

There is in Russian Bol'shevism a definite and precise mystical aspect.

Only having guessed at and having studied it, only having understood the mystical premises in Communist rule in Russia, is it definitely possible to say, whither it attempts to lead Russian culture, and what perhaps is opposed to it.

And indeed this new power, having its own definite cultural program, arose during a period, precisely when two impasses were delineated.

The impasse of the official Church, -- empirically having grown over into a shell, languishing beneathe the basket not enlightening the world with truth, having been brought to its undoing and impairment under bishop Barnabas and Rasputin.

And on the other side, -- human activity, whipped up by utopianism, thirsting after a religious justification for its doings, possessing merely a surrogate religion in the hypertrophied soaring of utopia, -- was thus brought to an impasse.

God-manhood was hopelessly betrayed.

And only in light of the present day is it possible to bless the Russian XIX Century, for that it both betrayed neither the Divine principle, nor the human.

In those days wherein the fullness of Divine truth was untouchably watched over as in a church reliquary. And wherein upon its godless paths mankind substantiated and affirmed its human freedom, the freedom of creative individuality, the freedom of the human person.

In light of the present day, this affirmation sounds like a blessing of thanks to the XIX Century.

And so, -- "the Great October". The destruction of the old world.

Truly destruction, insofar as the purpose of October is perhaps embodied, and the embodiment perhaps final.

The mystical aspect of Bol'shevism is characterised not by that it is godless.

In essence all humanism is godless. Beginning with the end of the Middle Ages, in the West we have a godless secular culture, so well and fruitfully engrafted onto Russia by Peter.

All human utopias of an ultimate time, having caught hold on Russia itself, almost all human creativity, -- was godless, was outside of God.

This does not characterise Bol'shevism.

Basic to it, is that it is against-God.

For a first time they do not ignore God, but rather they go against God. For a first time anti-godliness is preached with a fiery passion.

For a first time "nothing" is set in opposition to God.

This anti-godliness, -- is one of the mystical obliterations of the Communist culture.

All this is particularly well known. It is necessary but to realise, that everyone is making a remarkable mistake in speaking not about anti-godliness, but merely about godless Communism.

When they talk about the godless, then they connect Communism together with the whole humanistic period of human culture, they make it somehow the culmination point of humanism, a reduction to the absurd.

But in this consists a very marked misunderstanding of the mystical aspect of Communism.

Struggling with all its might against the Divine principle, Communism with no less ardour struggles against the human principle.

Communism, -- just like it is a denial of the Church, so also is it a denial of humanism.

All the values, achieved by humanism, all the affirmation of human creativity, emancipated labour, freedom of conscience, public opinion, the idea of governance by the people, -- everything decisively, that was an accomplishment of the humanist period, everything to the same degree was trampled on by Communism.

The free human person is substituted for by a disciplined machine. Freedom of conscience is replaced by an all-compulsory social-philosophic doctrine. The struggle for free labour is prohibited and the factory has become a barracks. No sort of creativity can occur freely, if it does not have upon itself the seal of Communist creativity. The idea of governance by the people is replaced by compulsory dictatorship.

And this stamp has as its symbol the complete denial of free human creativity.

And so. Religion is trampled underfoot. The Divine principle is driven into the catacombs. In line with this the human principle also in suchlike measure and extent mustneeds go into the catacombs.

In the Soviet Solovetsk islands monks and revolutionaries live side by side. Soviet revolvers execute bishops and socialists the same.

A second mystical obliteration of Bol'shevism, -- is its anti-humanism, its against human aspect.

Simultaneously, systematically, deliberately, Bol'shevism carries on a struggle with both separate principles of God-manhood.

And mystically in this its dual tendency is an apparent truth. Communism, -- is a sinister and terrible punishment for the splintered image in the world of Christ the God man.

Its truth is in the culpability of the whole aggregate, -- the secular and spiritual culture of Russia. They cannot intersect and conjoin. They cannot create a synthesis.

And here now, -- they are denied and persecuted to the same extent.

What was not attained freely by will is now attained involuntarily, -- in the walled cellars of the Cheka or the Solovetsk: there is now conjoined, what was separated by centuries.

In any case they now augur the furthermost paths, upon which can be overcome the horrid present day.

And not only do they augur the paths, but also they mark the dangers, which can be met with upon them.

* * *

What pitfalls indeed await us tomorrow?

They are twofold. And their roots are in the twofold-split of yesterday, which perhaps still is not overcome.

On the one side is the human, utopian, godless creativity.

Those, who are on the other shore, -- on the shore of spiritual, church culture, -- hurl at it the reproach:

-- See, what ye have begotten. The present day of Communism, -- is flesh of your flesh and bone of your bones. Ye spake it, -- they wrought it. They -- are your logical conclusion.

And many on this shore would answer:

-- Yes, they are flesh of our flesh and bone of our bones. But our logical conclusion they are not, only a distortion. It is necessary to include rectifications, supplements, rational corrections. One decree would replace others, another would modify several, to set aright industriousness, to reach down to the peasantry, to acknowledge its needs, circumstances, etc.

In this answer is one of the possible pitfalls.

Such is the danger upon a purely human pathway.

In order to overcome it, it is first of all necessary to recognise, to what extent Communism is anti-man and anti-humanist. It is not flesh from flesh nor bone from bone, -- but rather a negation and a violation against the flesh and against the bone, and against the human spirit.

And alongside it is another danger, issuing from the opposite shore of Russian culture.

There they say: the godless humanist epoch outlives itself. Here indeed it has been taken to its logical conclusion, -- to the absurdity of Communism. Here indeed it has shown itself to us in all its stature as the kingdom of the Beast. Utopianism has shown its beastly face and its blood-stained hands ... Enough. History is set in the Parousia. Progress, -- is a fiction. The weeds grow up together with the wheat and it is not for us to pluck them out. Our affair, -- is to be concerned, that our grain-ears be full-weight for the Kingdom.

A wall is built, fencing off the Church from mankind. Human social creativity, moving by method of winged utopias, is declared the temptation of the Grand Inquisitor, and limit is put to the growth of the idea. There begins a period of personal spiritual perfection.

In other words, -- the demand for a repudiation of its very self is put to the world. The world mustneeds renounce its own laws, forget its own attainments, betray itself.

The great bon-fires of Savonarola, on which, in a new sort auto da fe will be burnt all the creative works of humankind in the area of its social thought.

Again and again in such manner runs the vicious circle. The squirrel of history continues to spin in the eternal race-wheel. The humanist epoch -- the epoch of human creativity and the affirmation of human freedom, -- is ended. In place of it comes that, which begat it.

God-manhood is betrayed anew. The flesh of Christ is forgotten. Divine Revelation is carried off from the world. Everything human is shoved beyond the church enclosure.

This is the second abyss, to which we are nigh.

*   *   *

What then is the true way?

It would seem, that the fierce chastisement of the against-godliness and the against-humanness which we now experience, -- is otherwise, it is against God manhood, and this precisely shows us the true way.

Not for the Divine principle and not for the human, -- not for a peopleless Church and not for humanism, but for God-manhood ought there now to be struggle.

Yes, in full measure and to the end to realise the cupola of the Church over oneself. In full measure and to the end to accept in mystery the fulness of Revelation. And at this time it is necessary in full measure and to the end to affirm and to bless not only the right, but indeed the duty of mankind to create its human deed.

All the branches of human creativity, -- science, art, society, -- and the state, -- are creations, searches for new winged utopias, the apperception of a single truth or a thousand truths, the struggle for the emancipation of labour, the affirmation of the right to work, the attempts of overall building up of societal life, -- popular rule, -- everything where there is a spark of collective or individual creativity, where individually or collectively human freedom is affirmed, and where man is obliged to be free, -- all this should be sanctified and blessed.

In a diminished and impaired form the human principle cannot be in contiguity with fullness.

Only all the fullness of human creativity, all the torment of its failure and all the delight of its attainment, -- only they alone are worthy to be united in God-manhood. Otherwise, even as a goal, God-manhood would be repudiated.

The empirical task appears for us to be a synthesis of culture, a struggle for wholeness of culture.

In it, and only in it is there a surmounting of the present day, in is appropinquity towards the true path, always, -- in measure of spiritual growth of the world, -- to its embodying by the idea of God-manhood.

The world awaits the birth of a new utopia, likewise winged, so that in its creative recovered-sight it would reveal to people the mystery of God-manhood. Then in concrete attainments, in the historical process, it would grant the world a synthesis of all the cultural freshets, a confluence within a single image of a now shattered and chaotic nature.

E. Skobtsova

TRANSLATOR POSTSCRIPT

To revisit one's past, over the span of a score of years ago, can be unsettling. Bittersweet the nuance of nostalgia, bright hopes crumbled to dust, dear souls seen to the grave, youthful dreams come to naught, amidst the harsh onrush of a pallid grey oblivion. How sobering the prospect, how sobering the thought. All to what end, or in vain? This present book, the English translation, was written and indeed typed into manuscript form 20 years ago, in 1996-1997, and found no willing publisher; thereafter it languished amidst "projects postponed until retirement", hence now or never...

Consider, in turn, the year 1929, when each of these four Skobtsova works was written. It was a mere decade and less from the massive trauma of the Revolution and the Russian Civil War, leaving a displaced Russian world lacerated in soul. How horrible the result, living as outcasts in foreign lands, trying to pick up the pieces of broken lives, to survive and to carry on, merely existing... And in 1929 the worldwide "Great Depression" ensued. A time indeed to try men's souls, a crushing time set to drive many to despair, to drink, to suicide. Somewhat later our authoress, as an untypical Orthodox monastic, as Mother Maria Skobtsova, via her "Orthodox Action" efforts, will address not theoretically but rather firsthand and directly this challenge. Yet already in our fourfold text there threads in common a motif, -- dare we revisit our painful past, dare we rekindle the dashed hopes and aspirations of our youth now beset in sober a maturity, dare we still to dreams of holy truth, of ernstwhile purpose and ideals, or in bitter regret consign all to naught, to oblivion, to no avail. An existential question, in even times not trying for men's souls.

E. Skobtsova (*Mother Maria*)

Mother Maria Skobtsova was born on 20 December 1891 [O.S. 8 December][1] as Elisaveta Pilenko; later Kuz'mina-Karavaeva by her 1st marriage, and Skobtsova by her 2nd marriage. And later, following monastic custom, she chose the name Maria. In her childhood, Skobtsova experienced a kindly side of the notorious K. Pobedonostsev[2], the civil head of the Holy Synod holding the Russian Church in thrall from addressing needed reforms. Typical of Russian intelligentsia youth of the time, she later became involved with the S-R's, the Social-Revolutionaries. As a poet participating in the St. Peterburg Silver Age cultural scene, she had a dalliance with the noted Russian Symbolist poet, Aleksandr Blok. Shortly after the Revolution, she became default mayor of Anapa in southern Russia, famously facing down a group of military would-be marauders. Within the emigration she settled in Paris in 1923, thereafter suffering a mother's grief at the death of a child, and the disintegration of her 2nd marriage (though remaining on cordial terms with Daniel Skobtsov). In 1932 Mother Maria "took the veil", becoming an untypical Orthodox nun, living an activist sort monasticism attending to those in woesome circumstances, -- her "Orthodox Action". During the wartime German occupation of France, Mother Maria was an active Resistance figure, sheltering Jews, forging baptismal certificates etc., and boldly attending to those rounded up in the notorious mass arrests and held at the Paris Sports Velodrome. Defiantly outspoken, she too in time was arrested, and died at the Ravensbrück concentration camp on 31 March 1945, by legend voluntarily taking the place of a Jewish woman. Mother Maria is recognised as among the righteous in Jewish memory of the Holocaust. And in the declining days of the Soviet Union there was

---

[1] Prior to the year 1900, during the XIX Century, 12 days separated the Calendars, unlike the 13 days at present.

[2] N. A. Berdyaev eulogised Pobedonostsev in a 1907 article entitled, "Nihilism on a Religious Soil".

even a movie made in Russia about Mother Maria (this too was a transitional time when Fr. Aleksandr Men' gave religious talks on Soviet television!). In 2004 Mother Maria Skobtsova was formally glorified to the ranks of the Saints by the Constantinople Patriarchate, rather than by the Moscow Church (on technical grounds of jurisdiction), -- in part perhaps masking the historical friction between Russian Paris and Moscow, sadly...

The year 1965 saw the publication of two biographies of Mother Maria Skobtsova. The first, and finer, was entitled: "The Rebel Nun: the Moving Story of Mother Maria of Paris", written by T. Stratton Smith (Souvenir Press, UK; Templegate, US). The second biography, by Fr. Sergei Hackel, was originally entitled: "One of great Price: the Life of Mother Maria Skobtsova" (Darton, Longman & Todd, UK). The 1981 reprint of this by St. Vladimir Press altered the title to "Pearl of Great Price".

More recently, Mother Maria is one of the examples discussed by Fr. M. Plekon in his 2004 book, "Living Icons" (Notre Dame Press, US). Also Fr. Aleksandr Men's posthumous 2008 tome, "Russian Religious Philosophy: 1989-1990 Lectures", has been published in 2015 English translation (frsj Publications). Fr. Men's final lecture in this book, devoted to Mother Maria, was given several days before his own untimely death in 1990.

Back in 1992, the Paris YMCA Press published in Russian a 2 volume set of articles by Mother Maria entitled: "Мать Мария". Some of these articles later appeared in English translation under the title: "Mother Maria Skobtsova: Essential Writings" (Orbis Books, 2003). Several articles by Mother Maria in English translation appear also under the Skobtsova section of the berdyaev.com website (n.b. any duplicates pre-date the Orbis edition).

Our present four writings written in 1929 by Mother Maria, however, seem not to have been reprinted in Russian since their original publication, and hence remain largely inaccessible for even the Russian reader. In 1929, the Skobtsova works on Khomyakov, Dostoevsky and Vl. Solov'ev were published by Paris IMKA Press in three small separate booklets; the chronological order of their appearance is not evident, perhaps simultaneous. Skobtsova's article "In Search of Synthesis" ["В поисках синтеза"] appeared in the № 16 (May) issue of Journal Put', c. 49-68.In the 1980's, both the Khomyakov and Vl. Solov'ev booklets were still available from the Paris IMKA Press (Editions Reunis), which the present translator had the good fortune to order and purchase. A photocopy of the Dostoevsky booklet was kindly provided by N. Shapiro of Princeton University Library; the Journal Put' article likewise by E. Silk of the St. Vladimir Seminary Library. As initially mentioned, this present English translation languished for 20 years collecting dust since 1996-1997. And it is doubly ironic, then, that in the following year 1998, the Moscow Patriarchate consolidated the entire corpus of Journal's Put' onto a single CD-Rom (priced at $100 US, impossible for a then Russian), and moreover kept this priceless treasure a closely guarded secret from the world. It is now no longer available. The present translator managed to purchase his legitimate copy back then, through channels. The 1990's were an unsettled time for Russia; hopefully perhaps, the Moscow Church can be persuaded to remedy this oversight....

Please note: the section numbering in Skobtsova's Khomyakov text has been retained as it appeared in the original Russian edition: the "III" heading is used twice, and there is a shift from Roman to Arabic numeral form between Section "V" and Section "6". This is likely an oversight on the part of Skobtsova, based on haste and not caught by the editor, rather than deliberate an artistic flourish.

Also please note, that each of these four 1929 works are signed at the end as authored by "E. Skobtsova". Why? It was not until 1932 that Skobtsova "took the veil" becoming a monastic, and hence "Mother Maria Skobtsova".

Our present title, "The Crucible of Doubts", seems apt, a connecting theme pervading these four works, as perchance also the state of soul of Skobtsova in writing them. It is inspired by an enigmatic and intriguing saying by F. Dostoevsky, -- "Through the crucible of doubts my hosanna hath passed" ["Черезъ горнило соинений моя осанна прошла"]. This "gornilo somnenii" is innate to all those who at heart are "Dostoevskian folk", ever beset in soul and in mind by the "accursed eternal questions", akin to the disquiet of the proverbial Rachel (Mt. 2:18). In his brief eulogy which opens our text, Berdyaev hints at this within Mother Maria Skobtsova herself, that "her religiosity was not of the tranquil sort", "something tragic"; this perception of the tragic aspect underlying the human condition threads also throughout Berdyaev's existential philosophy of the person.

The idiomatic word "eulogy", at its Greek root, means "to speak well of", to bespeak a praise of the deceased, glossing away all but the praiseworthy. We see a similar process at work typically within hagiography (having translated the vita of many a saint), wherein are glossed away all the hardships and rough edges, leaving but a residue of heavenly placid and pretty platitudes. Indeed, at the close of the Orthodox funeral service, among the words of the priest's "Prayer of Final Absolution" over the deceased is this, that "all those things which have proceeded from the weakness of his/her mortal nature *be consigned to oblivion*"... This however relates to the *eternalisation of memory* on different a plane, as well as a proper understanding of the mystical image/icon of the human person, perceived as created "in the image and likeness of God"; it does not nullify our earthly existence as naught. Otherwise, the human person is rendered flatly one-dimensional, rather than multi-faceted, as Mother Maria indeed was...

So, what sort of words to describe Mother Maria? Certainly not placidly angelic. If anything, she could be exasperating and dismaying, as she was for the several nuns and priest initially involved with her community, unable to adjust and focus on different a sort of monasticism. Stormy weather indeed. And at times an irritating vexation for her bishop. Bold, stubborn, intrepid, contentious, tenacious, whether in the face of hollow-worded hypocrisy, or actually directly doing "Orthodox action" rather than merely talking about the plight of the misfortunate, delegating it off to yet another self-enriching charity. How fecklessly brazen her boldness to penetrate the Paris Velodrome to provide assist to the so many Jews rounded up there by the Nazis. How defiantly courageous her Resistance activity in support of the Jews, earning her the path to her final earthly fate. She was of that sort of strong-willed woman who, while the menfolk talk and dabble a matter to death, herself seizes the initiate and makes it happen. Both in many a parish church community and many an household this is so: the real boss managing the household is the wife, with the husband accorded titular authority akin to that of the British monarchy. My beloved wife, now at eternal repose, was similar a strong-willed woman of initiative, and she and others of her generation looked to Mother Maria as kindred an example.

From her credentials as a Silver Age cultural figure and S-R intelligentsia member, Mother Maria was by no means lacking in education and intelligence. She was one of many from her generation within that strange metamorphosis of the Russian intelligentsia from godlessness back to God, to the Church, reflecting a deepening, not a betrayal, of inner convictions. And not as some mere formality, but vitally, a matter of every living breath. In Mother Maria we see that restlessness of the Russian soul, an inner agitation, an impatience with "this world" and its tinsel values, and little tolerance to compromise with contentment, with foppery. Her writing style is indicative of this -- short staccato sentences and paragraphs, like bursts from a machine-gun (so very unlike Berdyaev's trait of convoluted sentences and unending paragraphs). Women's minds do ever bewilder men, with the nuances of the unspoken beneathe the spoken, a feminine different twist of perspective, at times challenging and annoying as to the gist of the point, certainly does exist in Mother Maria. And can be vexatious at times to render her in translation (Fr Alvian Smirensky, a fellow Skobtsova translator, once also corroborated this).

Some examples from out translation of her articles. We all know, or should know the opening Beatitude, -- "Blessed are the poor in spirit, for theirs is the Kingdom of Heaven" (Mt. 5:3). But what does it mean to be "poor in spirit", what is this "poverty in spirit"?

Why did Christ preach such a strange thing? One would think that a "richness in spirit", a "wealth of spirit" moreso is needed to gainsay the Kingdom of Heaven. Christ here is not making some societal justice comment, He does not express it as "the poor", but rather as "*the poor in spirit*", another dimension entirely. Moreover, we might remember how that scoundrel Judas "loved the poor". Orthodox Christians hear these words from the Beatitudes at nearly every Liturgy, yet these enigmatic words remain largely unasked as to meaning, and worse still, largely unanswered by our erudite sorts bustling about over many other *more important* things, like the proverbial Martha... But here is Mother Maria grappling with it, like the proverbial Mary, Martha's sister. The refrain "for theirs is the Kingdom of Heaven" occurs again later in the Beatitudes concerning "those outcast for righteousness' sake", -- meaning what? Perhaps to live it is to know it... Mother Maria in her dissonance does not address the Beatitude, -- "Blessed are the meek, for they shall inherit the earth", -- but with a certain sense of irony she might concur, that this has already transpired, with the meek in the mold of C. Dickens' "Mr. Umble" character, having made a true muck of things; but we do seek other than "the earth"...

In Skobtsova's "Emulation of the Mother of God" article, we are treated to a truly amazing an insight and perception, -- those rows upon rows of crosses in WWI military cemeteries symbolically represent inverted crosses plunged within the ground, their hand-hilts forming the crossbeam of the cross. The symbolic "confluence of cross and sword". On one plane, the Cross of Christ, which He alone bore, and then too the cross as sword prophecy of Righteous Simeon to the Mother of God: "And for Thee Thineself a sword shalt pierce the soul" (Lk. 2:35). And how indeed are we to make sense of Christ's saying, that He is come to bring "not peace, but the sword" ["Не мните, яко приидохъ воврещи миръ на землю: не приидохъ воврещи миръ, но мечь"] (Mt.10:34)? It is not an invocation to shedding torrents of blood, but rather to a radical transvaluation of values, discerned perchance in that "poverty of spirit"...

In various of her articles, Mother Maria has the knack of bringing in a woman's view, a woman's perspective and twist. Whether in the articles on the Mother of God, or otherwise regarding the Sin-Fall, along with Adam there was also Eve, both in their unique ways facing the challenge of God-manhood...

As regards our present text, what worth and relevance if any is there to it? Consider first the Khomyakov portion. His concept of Kushite creative dynamism is intriguing, -- from what aspect and period of Persia/Iran he derives this, would be interesting to discern (perhaps Berdyaev's 1912 "Khomyakov" book might elaborate, when the translation appears). And then too there is Khomyakov's populist almost anarchist unique Slavophil grounding for the autocracy. But Khomyakov's greatest legacy lies in the concept of "Sobornost'", which has so entered into the currency of Orthodox Christian thought and discussion. Sobornost' is often translated as "communality", distinct from mere "community", reflecting a socio-spiritual coherence. It provides an authentic basis of true human brotherhood, so different from the socialist substitute of tovarisch/comrade, as Berdyaev variously notes. A tovarisch is a comrade only so long as he is of use to you, otherwise expendable and terminal. Sobornost' is sometimes translated as "catholicity", deriving from the Slavic adjective "sobornyi", "catholic", in the liturgical Nicene Creed. What is the meaning of "to be catholic", as are Orthodox Christians, yet apart from Rome and its views? Sometimes Sobornost' gets translated as "conciliarity", from the root word "sobor" meaning both "cathedral" and "council". It is a significant concept which has affected discussions of ecclesiality of recent years, not only in the Eastern but also the Western Church. Yet in the literature, sobornost' often gets consigned into a static jingoistic slogan, short on depth.

Is Sobornost' a static reality, or dynamic a process? Stasis as a state of being is proper to a corpse, a thing, less so to a living being. If dynamic a process, wherein precisely is the greatest point of focus in its actualisation? Consider the Orthodox Liturgy, as it builds in dynamic an intensity, we find exhortations to *"edinomyshlenie"* (oneness of mind) and *"edinoserdie"* (oneness of heart, i.e. accord, concord), as we approach invoking the Holy Spirit in the Epiklesis, then the "Our Father", and finally the climax of partaking the Eucharistic Gifts of the Son. This too is a vivifying actualisation of Vl. Solov'ev's "God-manhood" at its most intense, -- the personal re-encounter of the human person with the Divine Persons of the MostHoly Trinity. The liturgy is of course the most intense instance of the Christ-invoking "where two or three are gathered together in My Name" (Mt. 18:20), -- of being "in communion" with God. Is the Trinity in a stasis of perfection, akin to some unliving thing or ideal forms, or is it rather in a dynamism of perfection? St. Peter confesses, "Thou art the Christ, the Son of the *Living* God" (Mt. 16:16). And Christ teaches: "God is not the God of the Dead, but of the *living*" (Mt. 22:32). Amidst the dynamic life of the living Divine Persons of the Trinity there likewise obtains this oneness and unanimity of Sobornost', perfectly so. Sobornost' is radically and far different a process from that of a democratic majority vote sort of thing; it is far more profound a dynamic within experience, grounded in spiritual depth, and not trite political expediency.

Skobtsova's Dostoevsky tome -- comprises as it were an "Essential Dostoevsky", all in a concise brief compendium. It is all there, all the succinct motifs and schemes and themes. The spirit of the Grand Inquisitor and his "improved Christianity" and methods. Echoed in Shigalev's madly real program of revolutionary societal manipulation cycles playing out in the recent past and even moreso today. Who in their inmost heart, assuming it not too dulled and deadened, cannot be moved by Ivan Karamazov's assertion, to refuse his ticket either to heaven or to some future utopian universal harmony, bought at the price of a single tiny tear of some abused child beating itself upon the breast crying out vainly to its God... This is a radical positing of the problem of theodicy, not readily resolved; we might allow that Christ-God somehow takes upon Himself our sufferings, the sense of compassionate co-suffering, well and good for ourself as sober adults, but why for that child, for that child to suffer... How can we not but be moved by utmost revulsion at a world where this obtains not just for one, but for so very many, too so very many children, not merely from human stupidity, but from natural causes like sickness and disease... Here indeed is that "Crucible of Doubts" that will either crush our fragile faith, or else deepen it.

And within Dostoevsky there variously recurs that indeed devilish suggestion: "If there is no God, then all is permissible". We see this increasingly in our modern culture, even if not commonly taken to the extreme by Raskol'nikov. Demonic obsession, demonic monomania with an idea -- we see this with so many, be it Stavrogin, Kirillov, and others, caught up in a self-destroying nihilism. There is Ivan Karamazov, plunging towards a mental breakdown into madness, with a peculiar gift of seeing unseeing, akin to Christ's words "seeing they see not, and hearing they understand not" (Mk. 4:12). And there is that 4th Karamazov brother, true spawn of his father, the half-brother Smerdyakov, whose very name seems somehow cognate with the Russian word for death, -- "smert'". And can it be, that the very devil himself, is an agnostic concerning God... The final conversation with the seedily attired devil hints at this, as does indeed also the 2nd Temptation of Christ. Can we fail to mention that demented utopian dream of Versilov, of a mankind finally accepting that there is no God nor anything more, and finally left to themselves, they would warmly embrace and care each for the other. Bereft of the idea of immortality, there would remain "only the single tortuous pity for those like him, the certain pre-death fondness towards each blade of grass". How chillingly real this has become! And then too there is Verkhovensky's insight into the efficacy of shame, the "right to dishonour", which in our day gets termed "political correctness". And then there is Russia in its extreme contradictions as a "God-bearing people", a Russia in which the visage of woman oscillates between that of the Madonna and that of the sodomic, of Mary Magdalene, of Mary of Egypt. And then too there is Shatov, when asked by Stavrogin whether he believes in God, replies -- "I believe in Russia", and asked again the same, Shatov replies -- "I *shall believe* in God". And in this, how readily the word "church" can be substituted for "Russia", and not only in Russia...

And yet, in Dostoevsky there is not an hopeless black pessimism, as might seem warranted, but rather a subtle nuance of optimism, beneathe all the grime of human life, an optimism based on faith in the God, Whose ways are inscrutable. We see this towards the end with Raskol'nikov, with Dmitri Karamazov and others, where the end is not the final end. Consider the all too true statement of Fr. Zosima: "They purport to build up justly, but having renounced Christ, they will finish up by this, that they will inundate the world with blood, wherein blood crieth out for blood... If there were not the promise of Christ, then would they so hew one another down to the very last two men upon the earth". How chillingly prophetic! That monastic elder, the starets Zosima, the radiant Zosima mirroring the radiant visage of Christ and of God's love, that small glimpse of the radiant feast of faith via Alyosha, -- how so very different from the twisted glowering love personified in the monk Ferapont, Zosima's monastic nemesis, whose distortive caricature of faith and love we meet with so commonly often. For many of us, in reading Dostoevsky in our youth, Fr. Zosima is our first exposure to this venerable institution within Orthodoxy, that of the monastic starets/elder endowed with a spiritual gift of insight into the soul and heart of those seeking counsel. This graced ability of insight, or perspicacity (prozorlivost'), is a spiritual charism given to some not all the saints (whose vitae we once translated). Of course, one mustneeds judge a tree from its fruit, or lack thereof. Even in our modern secular culture, we have the abundant example of people flocking to whatever be the guru of the day considered chic, yielding possibly lucrative a career. Anciently within Christianity this begat gnosticism. And then too, from our non-religious modernity, consider this absurdity: the father of the modern science of psychology, Freud, did not believe in the existence of that his science literally proclaimed to be of -- "psukhe-logia" -- which from Greek translates as "science of the soul". And yet, in summation, Dostoevsky himself possessed a peculiar creative gift and talent of prophetic insight, the unique ability of authentic a seer with pervasive a perspicacity, to penetrate down beneathe the surface aspect of ideas to their ultimate, all too often, fruition.

Vladimir Solov'ev was proclaimed as Russia's first national philosopher of note a few mere years after his death (thereafter, true, becoming another Soviet non-person). There is a strange coincidence and significance too little noted, in that Vl. Solov'ev and F. Nietzsche both died at the turn of the century in the year 1900 -- the former on 13 August and the latter on 15 October. There is an aesthetic element unique to both. For Solov'ev, this derived from his visions of the heavenly Sophia, in the visage of a divinely Beauteous Woman, an eternal feminine element attributable to the Divinity, bringing to mind Goethe's Faust closing line concerning the "Ewig Weibliche". The Greek-derived word Sophia in Russian is "Mudrost'" or more properly in context "Premudrost'", i.e. literally verymost or utmost Wisdom. Vl. Solov'ev's intuition of Sophia has had twofold a legacy: aesthetically as a motif within the Russian Symbolist poetry and literature, and secondly, as an entire discipline within Russian religio-philosophic thought. In part, this tends to represent a continuity of Neo-Platonist Idealism admixtured with modern feminist a wont. And partly the victim of churchly political intrigue both among his Paris colleagues and far off Moscow, Fr. S. Bulgakov in his ponderously profound works took Sophia to perhaps the point of hypostatic distortion regarding God in the Trinity. Berdyaev follows far different a path regarding Sophia, apart from the general trend within Sophiology, a legacy moreso on the periphery rather than in the mainstream.

Vl. Solov'ev's rather more significant contribution to Russian religio-philosophic thought, his perhaps greatest legacy, rests upon this, that he restored to awareness of a Christological seemingly long since "dead dogma", buried beneathe the dust of centuries, concerning the "God-Man" [Bogochelovek] Christ, and hence derivatively of "God-manhood" [Bogochelovechestvo]. There are some of an academic mindset, weakly schooled in historical Christianity, who balk at translating this term literally, and instead tend to render it bereft its source as some sort of "Divine Humanity" in pan-entheistic or pan-psychic a setting. This but muddies waters. Solov'ev's terminology tends to be philosophically obtuse, as does much of Russian religio-philosophic thought, schooled in German philosophy -- Schelling, Hegel, Kant, J. Boehme -- yet distinct from it in its soul; whilst a certain ultra-Orthodox element would prefer to disdain the entire discipline in preference of a mythically pure Byzantism. In Russia during Vl. Solov'ev's life began the noble work of "icon restoration" -- cleansing the murky candle-soot long blackened icons to reveal the vibrantly vivid colours of the originals. Intellectually, Vl. Solov'ev did similar a great service regarding the IV OEcumenical Council at Chalcedon in the year 451. Chalcedon addressed the "Hypostatic Union" of the two natures -- perfect by nature God and perfect by nature Man -- within the Divine Person [Hupostasis, Lichnost'] of Jesus Christ. The Chalcedon definition is couched in four negative terms, apophatically, i.e. of unfathomable mystery. We discuss this at greater length in our Postscript to Berdyaev's "Philosophy of Inequality". St. John Damascene somewhere or other points out that if Christ-God had not been truly born human also by-nature at the Incarnation, then Christ's salvific death on the Cross would have been in vain (since "what is not taken upon is not saved"). From the Genesis Creation account we learn that man is "created in the image and likeness of God", and from the Gospel Sermon on the Mount we learn of our filial/sonship relationship to God "Our Father"... God-manhood relates not only to Christ but implicitly in turn to us -- to the existential grounding of the concrete individual person in facing life, in the value structure that we choose to live by. This is the basis for a Christian existentialism, transcending the isolation and alienation characteristic of our objectified material reality.

Vl. Solov'ev in his own quixotic way proved to be one of the fore-fathers of the modern Ecumenical movement within Christianity, the fruit of which has been both good and bad, since "the devil is always in the details". Solov'ev's "Anti-Christ Tale" from within the "Three Conversations" bears reading. Towards the end of his life had no fixed abode, and died at the house of a friend, as though in example of Christ's words (Mt. 8:19-20).

Skobtsova's Journal Put' article, "In Search of Synthesis", in brief, might be summarised thus: God-manhood is the ideal, whereas the starkly real is man-godhood. We find mention already in Dostoevsky of the phrase "man-godhood", in a discussion of Kirillov with Stavrogin. We tend to think of the word synthesis in terms of dialectics, a resolution between thesis and antithesis, hence the need for a concretely existential philosophic and psychological wholeness, integrality [tselost'], i.e. vital meaning. Is there any true synthesis possible, is something that the reader himself must seek to answer...

The original draft of this Postscript, 20 long years ago, dwelt much on the concept of "appropinquity", i.e. of proximity or connecting closeness. Mother Maria, Berdyaev and other creative lights of their generation, and preceeding generations, were intimately involved with and attentive to sources. A parallel effect exists within Christianity in the example of the "Apostolic Fathers": that early generation who in their youth sat at the feet of the Holy Apostles hearkening firsthand to their words, those selfsame Holy Apostles who earlier in turn sat directly at the feet of Christ, hearkening to His words and teaching. Herein lies a basis of both proximity and continuity, of a tradition, one in which we vitally participate. The alternative is to distance ourselves, in the name of some sort of a scientific academic detachment of objective approach which so often, as Christ observes, obtains that "seeing they see not, and hearing they hear not, and understand not" (Mt. 13:13)...

In summary, this translation is the result of a chance meeting, an encounter -- another appropinquity. Back in the mid 1990's the translator as a parent accompanied his son's class trip to Washington DC and also the Holocaust Museum there. In the Holocaust Museum -- endless images of unknown strangers, endless horrors, endless tragedies, and at the end of this a gallery of images of those who perished, and among these too terribly many faces of hapless souls nearly the first seen is a familiar face -- Mother Maria Skobtsova. It is from roughly this period in his life that the translator began translating in earnest, initially hagiography, then Russian religious philosophy. Whether this constitutes a proper miracle to Mother Maria's credit or not, God knows. But this present volume in effect closes a circle of memories, and repays a debt of gratitude nonetheless. Back then, 20 long years ago, it was proper to invoke prayerful remembrance of Mother Maria Skobtsova with the words: "Memory Eternal" ["Vechnaya Pamyat'"]. But now, with Mother Maria Skobtsova having been formally enumerated to the ranks of the Saints, it is more felicitous to say:

Holy Monastic Mother Maria, pray God for us!
Преподобная Матька Мария, моли Бога о нас!
Prepodobnaya Mat'ka Maria, moli Boga o nas!

April 2016
Fr. Stephen Janos

frsj Publications

1.) **N. A. BERDYAEV** *"The Philosophy of Inequality"*
   1st English Translation of Berdyaev's 1918/1923 book,
   "Filosofia neravenstva" (Kl. № 20).
   (ISBN-13: 978-0-9963992-0-3 / ISBN-10: 0-9963992-0-8)
   406 pages (6/4/15)

2.) **N. A. BERDYAEV** *"The Spiritual Crisis of the Intelligentsia"*
   1st English Translation of Berdyaev's 1910 book,
   "Dukhovnyi krizis intelligentsii" (Kl. № 4).
   (ISBN-13: 978-0-9963992-1-0 / ISBN-10: 0-9963992-1-6)
   346 pages (6/19/15)

3.) **FR. ALEKSANDR MEN'** *"Russian Religious Philosophy: 1989-1990 Lectures"* -- 1st English Translation
   Published in 25th Year Commemoration of Fr Men' Memory
   (ISBN-13: 978-0-9963992-2-7 / ISBN-10: 0-9963992-2-4)
   214 pages (7/14/15)

*   *   *

Forthcoming Works in Preparation:

N. A. BERDYAEV *"The Fate of Russia"* (Kl. № 15).
   1st English Translation of Berdyaev's 1918 *"Sud'ba Rossii"*.

N. A. BERDYAEV *"Aleksei Stepanovich Khomyakov"*
   1st English Translation of Berdyaev's 1912 book,
   "Алексей Степанович Хомяков" (Kl. № 6).